A QUEER LITTLE HISTORY OF ART

ALEX PILCHER

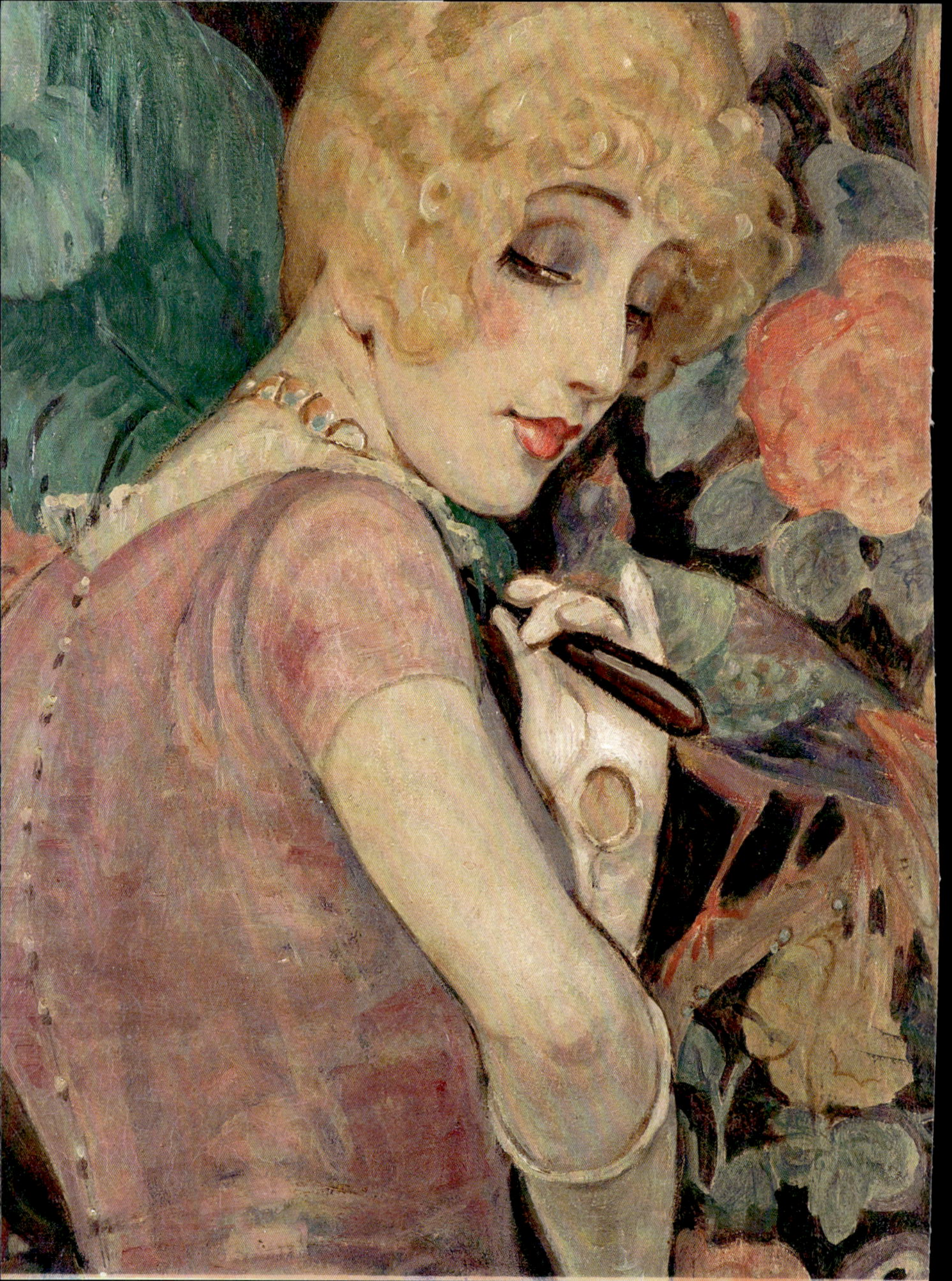

A QUEER LITTLE HISTORY OF ART

ALEX PILCHER

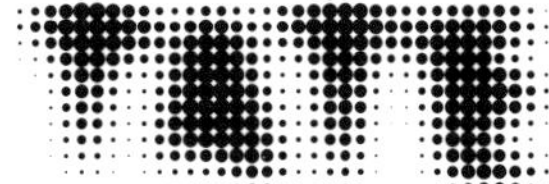

First published 2017 by order of the
Tate Trustees by Tate Publishing,
a division of Tate Enterprises Ltd,
Millbank, London SW1P 4RG

www.tate.org.uk/publishing

© Tate Enterprises Ltd 2017

Reprinted 2018, 2019, 2021, 2022, 2023, 2025

A catalogue record for this book is available from the
British Library

ISBN 978-1-84976-503-9

Distributed in the United States and Canada by
ABRAMS, New York

Library of Congress Control Number:
applied for

Designed by Untitled
Colour reproduction by DL Imaging, London
Printed and bound in Spain by SYL L'ART GRÀFIC
PREMIUM

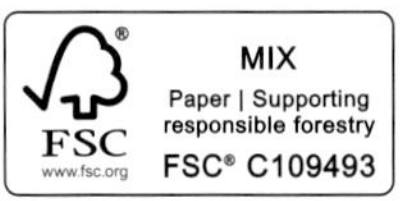

Front cover: Tee A. Corinne *Untitled* 1976,
published 1977. See pp. 90–1

Back cover: Alexej von Jawlensky *Portrait
of the Dancer Alexander Sakharoff* 1909.
See pp. 24–5

Frontispiece: Gerda Wegener *Lili With a Feather Fan*
1920. See pp. 40–1

Measurements of artworks are given
in centimetres, height before width

In this book, the author uses the singular gender-
neutral pronouns 'they', 'their' and 'them' for historical
figures whose lives suggest a turn away from their
assigned gender. This isn't to assert that these
individuals were expressly 'non-binary' – in terms we
understand today – or to preclude other identities. It
is a rough device to avoid erasing the possibility that
they experienced their gender in ways we might now
label 'trans'.

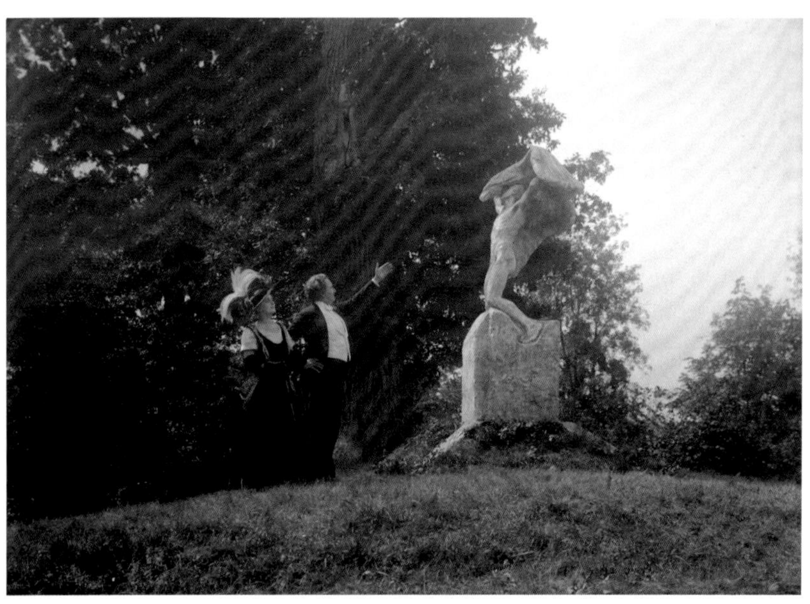

INTRODUCTION

Scene One – *A hilltop, evening*. Two figures in elegant costumes have climbed here to view a work of art. They stand before a sculpture of a naked youth, on his knees below a giant eagle. The image is from a film made in Sweden in 1916 (opposite). Directed by Mauritz Stiller (1883–1928), *The Wings* ('Vingarne') is the fictional tale of artist Claude Zoret – seen here trying to impress a potential client with his latest work.

Why choose this shot from a largely forgotten silent film to begin a book about modern and contemporary art? Unlikely as it sounds, Mauritz Stiller's early feature touches the heart of this book's theme: the fertile interrelationship between art and the modern queer experience. *The Wings* is the earliest known film about a same-sex relationship. Zoret's romantic feelings are focused on his beautiful protégé, Eugène Mikaël – also the model for the sculpture on the hilltop. The unique bronze cast of the latter is given to Mikaël by the doting artist and the sculpture's fate is entangled with Zoret's unhappy end.

Zoret's story is taken from an earlier novel named *Mikaël* by Danish author Herman Bang (1857–1912), who made his artist character a painter. The film's departure from its queer literary source is accounted for in its peculiar framing plot. *The Wings* starts off as a film about the *making* of a film, also titled 'The Wings'. The prologue tells us that the sculpture used in the film is actually the work of a contemporary Swedish

Still from *The Wings* ('Vingarne') (dir. Mauritz Stiller, AB Svenska Biografteatern, Sweden 1916)

artist, Carl Milles (1875–1955, see also pp.42–3). In the opening scene, playing himself, Stiller announces that Milles' sculpture will be the germ of his next movie. The film even borrows the sculpture's title, in preference to that of Bang's novel. So what is it about *The Wings* that helped inspire this early venture into queer cinema?

Carl Milles modelled several versions of *The Wings* from 1908 onwards, ranging from statuette to monumental scale. One full-size bronze cast was purchased by the state in 1911 and holds a prominent position on Stockholm's waterfront, before the National Museum. Stiller's film revolves around a work of modern art that, to local audiences, was easily recognisable.[1]

The sculpture may have been modern, but it draws on a myth roughly three thousand years old: the love of Zeus, chief god of the Greeks, for a mortal named Ganymede. All who beheld Ganymede were enthralled by this young man's beauty. Zeus was no exception, and on this occasion, the divine shape-shifter takes the form of an eagle to pursue the object of his lust. Ganymede is snatched from a hillside in Phrygia (in modern-day Turkey) and taken to live among the gods on Mount Olympus. It's hard to imagine any story setting a more elevated precedent for erotic desire between men. The Athenian philosopher Plato even suggested the whole thing had been made up by the people of Crete to provide a divine cover story for their own sexual habits. The object of Zeus's affection became a byword for men who had sex with men. From ancient Rome right up to the industrial age, the name Ganymede and its Latin derivative *catamite* often served as terms for the younger or prettier of two male partners.

There were other ancient myths of same-sex attraction, but Ganymede's story was the most enduring vehicle for such desires in European art.

The heartthrob appears on Greek painted pottery of
the fifth century BC and on the frescoed walls of ancient
Roman houses. Ganymede even pops up in medieval
Christian manuscript illustrations. Yet he really takes
off in early sixteenth-century Italy. Michelangelo
(1475–1564) pictured a naked Ganymede swooning
in the grip of a masterful eagle (p.10) and, just like
Claude Zoret in *The Wings*, presented his version to the
beautiful young man who had inspired it. His much-
copied drawing set the tone for dozens more languid
Ganymedes scattered throughout three hundred
years of Western art.

The nude figure in Milles' sculpture is a direct
descendant of Michelangelo's airborne adolescent.
This modern Ganymede grasps the giant bird with
both arms, eager to be swept away by his feathered
lover. Queer yearning is conveyed here in discreet
guise, relying on a smattering of classical education
to be understood. From the rise of Christianity until
the late nineteenth century, same-sex desires were
rarely endorsed in European art other than through
such coded references to ancient myths or biblical
narratives. Aspects of human experience that modern
societies reviled as sinful, criminal or pathological
could only be safely romanticised in a faraway past.
That was about to change.

The Wings stands at a crossroads in queer culture.
The tradition of veiled homoerotic imagery that led
up to the sculpture by Carl Milles was already on the
wane. The modern-day storyline of Stiller's film is an
indication of what would emerge in its stead. In the
art of the last hundred years, queer sexualities and
genders have discarded classical drag. Whether in the
arts, activism or popular culture, contemporary queer
lives have become unapologetically visible. It's a shift
being played out in urban societies around the world –

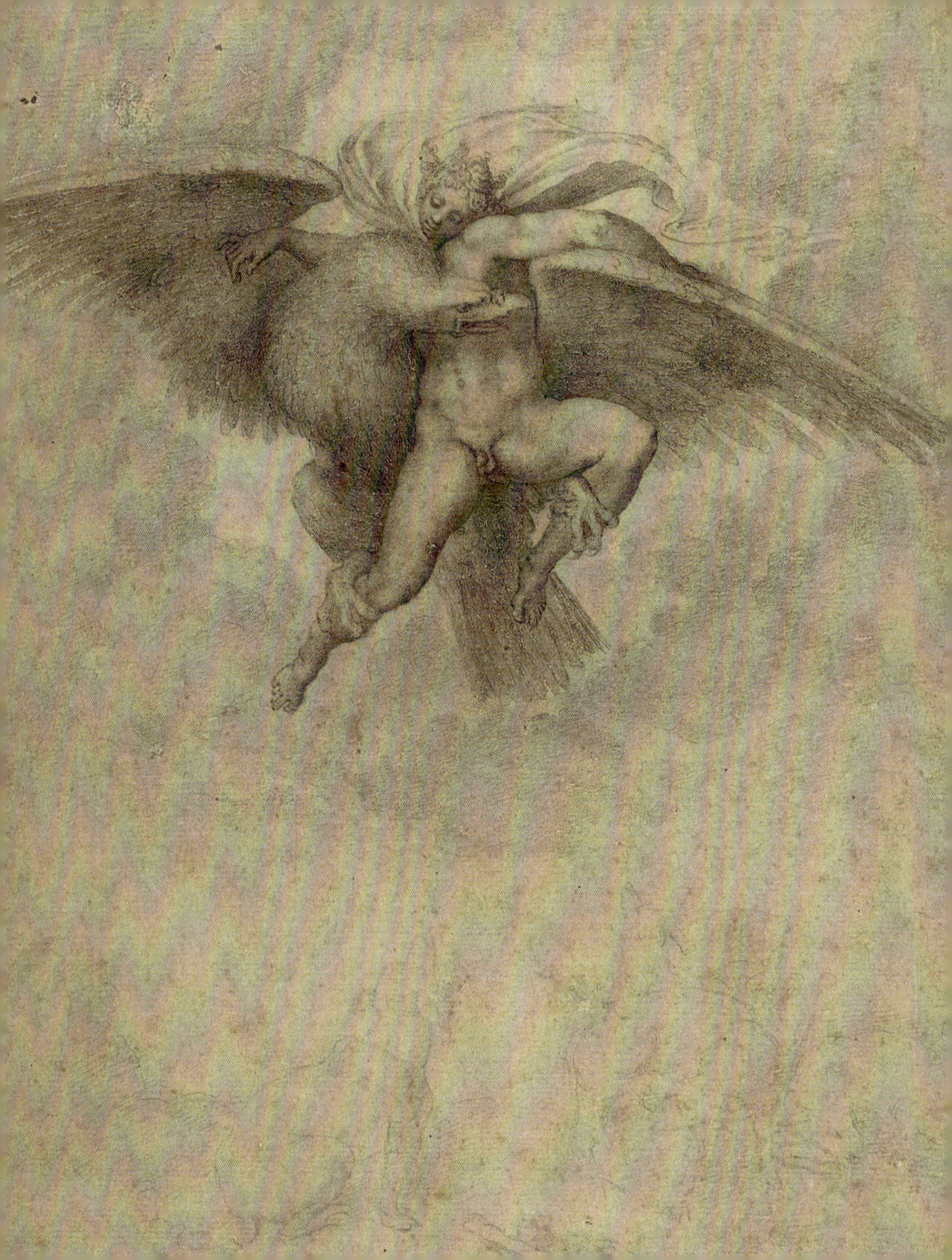

with rich local variations. Perhaps that sounds unduly upbeat when so many societies continue to severely punish those who breach local norms of gender, love or sexual expression. Even in countries with laws designed to ensure equality for all, freedoms are fully enjoyed by the most privileged only. Nevertheless, the social changes of the past century are not illusory and we should remember they were neither inevitable nor easily won. Most of the artists included in these pages took considerable risks through their lives and their art alike. Putting together this collection has been, in part, a way of paying tribute to their boldness.

Why queer art history?

As a term, 'queer' has incited a bewildering amount of debate and redefinition, claim and counter-claim and it seems only fair to explain why I opt for using the word in this book. The label has a history of being spoken in hatred – many of us remember being on the receiving end of it as a term of abuse – but from the mid 1980s onwards there has been a defiant move to reclaim the word queer. It has lent its name to club nights and activist groups, TV shows and community projects. It has spawned its own academic discipline of 'queer studies', underpinned by an often-daunting body of 'queer theory'. The word has been coupled with almost every topic you could imagine. Art history is one of countless fields that have developed 'queer' offshoots.

There's no space here to unravel all the definitions that 'queer' has inspired in recent years, but there are three that have widespread currency. Queer, first of all, is frequently employed as an 'umbrella' term: a word encompassing anyone who could be described as lesbian, gay, bisexual, asexual, transgender, third gender or intersex. It offers a snappier alternative to such unloved acronyms as 'LGBTQIA+'. Secondly, many individuals in Western societies have championed queer as an identity in its own right. Asserting one's position as 'queer' can feel like a defiant stance in the face of emerging forms of gay or trans respectability that seem to leave more marginalised groups behind. Mainstream acceptance of LGBT people has been extended incrementally and grudgingly. It tends to come with conditions attached, applying implicit standards to our appearance, styles and behaviours, splitting LGBT people into 'good' and 'bad' flavours. Queer activist movements typically reject such hierarchical distinctions, along with commercialised visions of LGBT life. Queer-identified communities tend to celebrate variety in sexual lifestyles, relationship choices, body types, gender identities and styles of expression.

The third sense of queer I want to highlight goes back to the word's older usage: describing something as odd or strange. Like those two adjectives, queer has no intrinsic essence. It is not a specific category but a deviation from what is perceived as a norm. This makes it both slippery and potentially subversive. We have become used to a model of lesbian and gay identities coexisting with a default heterosexuality – a serene multiculturalism of desire. 'Queer' gives a name to what this model leaves out. It demands to know, what's so 'normal' about heterosexuality? What are we excluding when we picture our sexual 'orientations' as fixed and consistent?

Actual desires refuse to be rigidly governed by our twentieth-century models of sexuality. Our genders also have an anarchic streak. Many of us spend a fair portion of our lives failing to stick to the gender script we were assigned. Anomalies of gender and desire are so familiar that they have inspired an armoury of clichés designed to tame them. '*Everyone* is a bit

bisexual *really*.' '*All* girls go through a tomboy phase.'
'A *well-adjusted* man is in touch with his feminine side.'
A queer outlook declines to tidy away our deviations with
minor adjustments to the prevailing norms. When we are
thinking queerly, those norms themselves are called into
question. What does it mean to be 'bisexual really' if that's
not how one thinks of oneself? Can a person have more
than one sexuality at once? How is it that girls who prefer
to look 'boyish' at six are viewed as cute, while those who
look boyish at sixteen arouse concern? Where exactly
do men's 'feminine sides' begin and end? Do they have
'masculine sides' as well? The more queer paths we head
down, the less credible our norms start to appear.

These definitions of queer are interrelated. All three
helped guide the selection of the artworks in this book,
which date from 1900 to now. Among the artists included,
some identify with queer in the politicised sense of the
word. Many more belong under the queer umbrella.
Yet art that represents the world queerly may be found
much further afield. If we allow works of art their own
voice – independent of the identities and life histories of
their makers – we need not treat queer art as a territory
with fixed borders. I have sought out art that suggests
non-normative visions of gender or sexuality, though
this takes me beyond the familiar roster of LGBT artists.
The queerness of these artworks will be obvious in some
cases, but elsewhere, coded or ambiguous. It may be
central to the aims of certain artists, and an unlooked-for
effect in the work of others.

This book is not the story of an art movement. It does
not map a distinctive queer style. It is emphatically not
a parade of artists linked by a particular characteristic.
If you are expecting to find a handbook of 'queer artists'
then you may be disappointed. Revealed here are some
of the ways art has explored queer experience: forms
of sexuality, eroticism, gender identities and styles

of expression that depart from society's norms. Of course, dominant assumptions about gender and desire change over time and vary enormously between cultures of the world. What appears queer in one setting may seem unremarkable in another. I have included art that feels queer from my perspective, but I should stress it's a perspective attuned to Western norms. By including artists working at considerable geographic and cultural distances from my own North European context – such as Ma Liuming (pp.106–7), Mrinalini Mukherjee (pp.114–15) or Tomoko Kashiki (pp.146–7) – I accept I may be appropriating their artworks to serve my localised queer agenda. This is not the only area of difficulty when it comes to reading art queerly.

Art gallery gaydar

If you have ever taken classes in art history, you may have been taught how to identify indigenous gods in Aztec art or to recite stages in the evolution of modern abstract painting. Something we are less often taught is how to trace a history of queer expression in art. In fact, teachers, art historians, museum curators and other guardians of knowledge have been known to make this harder. Take artwork titles, which by no means always stem from the artist. Curators and cataloguers often attach romantic tags – 'The Lovers' is a typical choice – to any pair of figures that can be read as a heterosexual couple. Comparable images of same-sex intimacy have been treated quite differently by generations of art historians. A veil is often drawn over the romantic or erotic possibilities of such artworks by the titles they have gone on to acquire: 'The Friends', 'Two Nudes', 'Double Portrait', 'Sisters'.

Important biographical information about artists has too often been excised altogether, downplayed or else interpreted in terms that fit with a presumption of heterosexuality. The same-sex partner becomes the 'close friend'; the artistic comrade is made out as the heterosexual love interest. Queerness that is beyond denial may still be neutralised in discussions of artists, even by well-informed authorities. Be prepared to find gay artists diagnosed as 'celibate', 'asexual' or 'sexually confused', without persuasive evidence. Such pet theories seem more palatable to some authors than the image of an artistic hero actually getting it on with someone of the same gender.

Similarly, a presumption of normative gender identity tends to skew accounts of certain artists. We will return to Gluck (pp.46–7), Toyen (pp.54–5) and Marlow Moss (pp.66–7). Each developed a rigorously masculine or androgynous self-presentation. Faced with such gender ambiguity, writers are still prone to explain it as simply a lesbian style choice – even as a career strategy for competing in a male-dominated field. Deeply felt gender variance, when considered at all, is generally treated as the least likely explanation. Before the late twentieth century, transgender identities were hardly ever clearly articulated in terms we would recognise today. That does not mean gender variance played any less of a role in queer experience. The queerness of Gluck, Moss or Claude Cahun (pp.48–9) is beyond debate; whether it is better read through a 'lesbian' lens or a 'trans' one is a question we cannot usefully settle. My preference is to keep both possibilities open and not to assume that one must exclude the other.

With much traditional scholarship serving to obscure the queer presence in art history, a common queer response is, simply, to use our eyes. In 2007, contemporary artist Henrik Olesen (b.1967, pp.120–1) held an exhibition in Switzerland, titled *Some Gay–Lesbian Artists and/or Artists Relevant to Homo-Social*

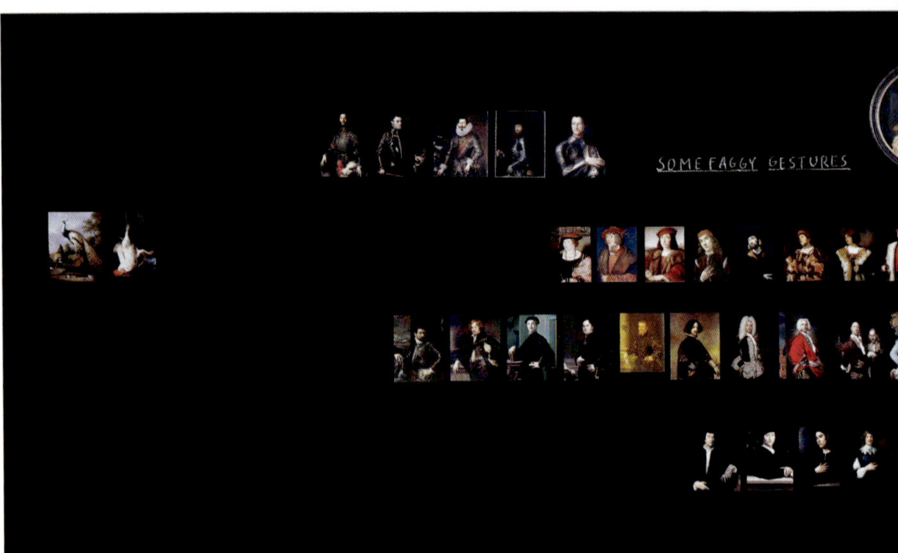

Henrik Olesen

Some Faggy Gestures 2007
Collage with computer prints
on board
140 x 600.1
Migros Museum, Zürich

Culture Born between c.1300–1870.[2] In a grand effort to promote a queerer understanding of art history, Olesen plastered display boards with images of hundreds of works of art, interspersed with text and historical information. One panel gathered portraits of high-status male sitters from the fifteenth to the eighteenth century, under the heading, 'Some Faggy Gestures' (above). With their limp wrists, soulful gazes, curling fingers and hands on hips, these gorgeously attired men do embody a certain gay stereotype – even if a rather dated one. Still, 'faggy' is surely not an accurate reading. The frilly costumes and swishy body language of the sitters follow masculine norms of their own day for men of their social class. Is 'Some Faggy Gestures' designed to license our anachronistic intuitions or to gently warn us of how error-prone they can be?

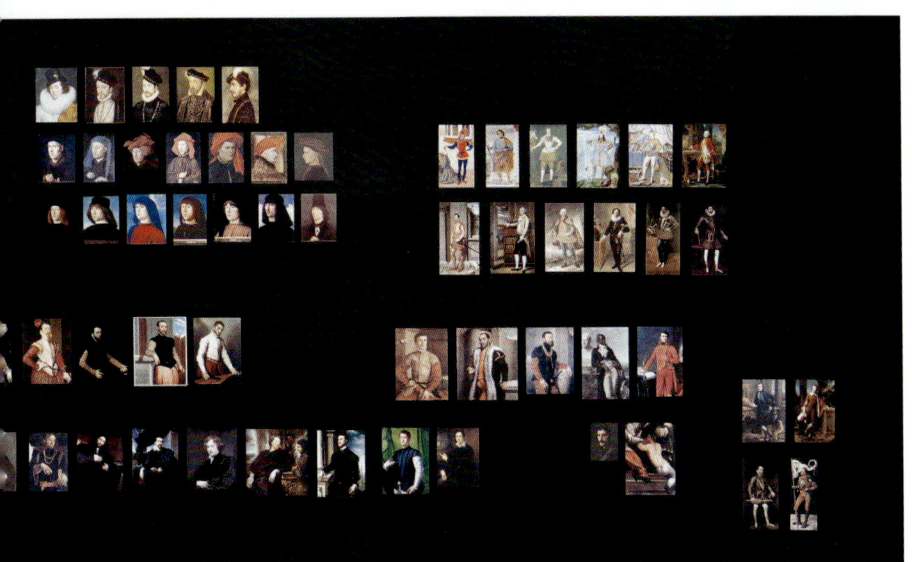

The game of spotting 'one of our own' can be a great source of queer pleasure in an art gallery. As a method of arriving at historical insight, it can be worse than useless. Olesen's montage smacks of gaydar gone rogue. But its manic repetition twists its visual argument in a queerer direction. 'Some Faggy Gestures' does not propose that these men or the artists who painted them were 'fags'. It reminds us that our concepts of 'faggy' and 'butch' are modern norms as opposed to timeless truths. The past can serve to reframe our present and highlight its historically contingent character. And art – which so often jars against our settled views of the world – provides a direct channel through which this can happen.

The challenges involved in reading art queerly don't go away when we turn to modern artists. Take, for example, a scene of two women by a riverside painted in 1928 by

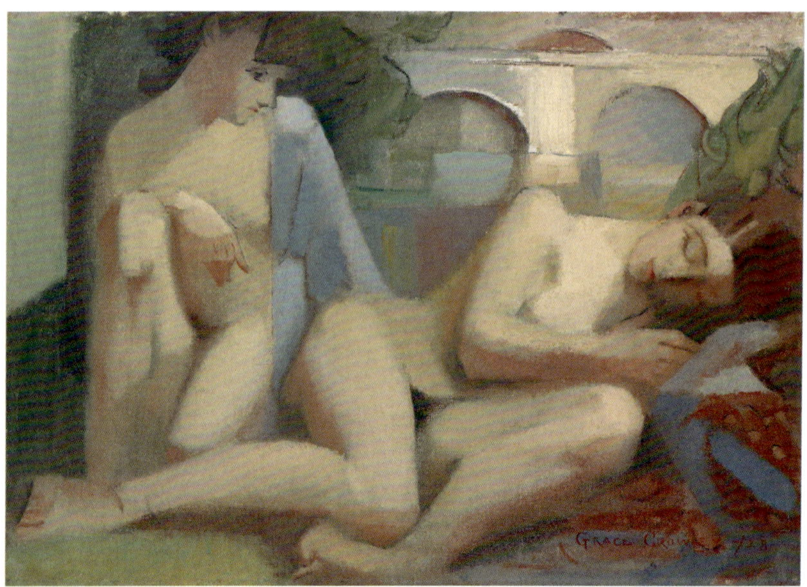

Grace Crowley
Les Baigneuses 1928
Oil paint on canvas on
composition board
45.2 x 64.2
National Gallery of Australia,
Canberra

Australian artist Grace Crowley (1890–1979) (above).
The kneeling figure at the left of *Les Baigneuses*
('The Bathers') takes advantage of her companion's
afternoon snooze to freely admire her naked body.
The suggestion of lesbian desire is surely intentional,
considering when and where the picture was made.
Crowley had arrived in Paris two years earlier to study
modern French art, enrolling at the private academy
run by André Lhote (1885–1962). The French capital at
this time was noted for its vibrant lesbian nightlife and
extensive networks of cultured queer women, many of
them foreign settlers. This helps explain why the theme
of lesbian couples became remarkably fashionable
among the large community of artists working in Paris
throughout the 1920s. Lhote was a prime exponent
of this trend. Crowley's bathers, with their softened

modernist outlines and Sapphic interrelationship, don't
differ greatly from figures in paintings by Lhote and his
other students. But does the gender of the artist boost
the queer status of the image? Is the gaze of Crowley's
kneeling bather more 'lesbian' than that of similar female
nudes painted by male artists?

Art theory of the last few decades has worked to
disentangle art from the personality and life history of
the artist: a reaction against the sentimental excesses
of romantic criticism. The meanings of an artwork are no
longer credited exclusively to the artist's intentions; the
active role of the spectator and the context of viewing
are now accorded more clout. Yet, the anti-biographical
direction of art theory clashes with most efforts to
develop a queer art history (including large chunks of this
book). To pick one obvious issue, the everyday concept
of 'homoerotic' art hinges as much on the gender of
the artist as on their subject matter (with the artist's
supposed sexuality often invoked to clinch the argument).

When even erotic, figurative art is hard to characterise
as queer without falling back on biographical data,
abstraction tests queer art history to the limit. New York-
based artist Keltie Ferris (b.1977) makes large abstract
paintings, often applying her bright colours with a spray
gun. Her titles are rarely easy to decipher, but perhaps
she threw down a gauntlet in naming one canvas *Gaydar*
(p.20). Could Ferris, who is gay, be teasing viewers over
their reflex urge to detect a gay 'look' in art made by gay
people? Certainly her title can be interpreted as a tongue-
in-cheek challenge: 'Try reading *this*!'

Networks of identity

It should be clear by now that queer art history is a rocky
terrain. I don't expect this book to tread its path without a
misstep. I have attempted to keep the focus on the works
of art themselves rather than the histories, genders or

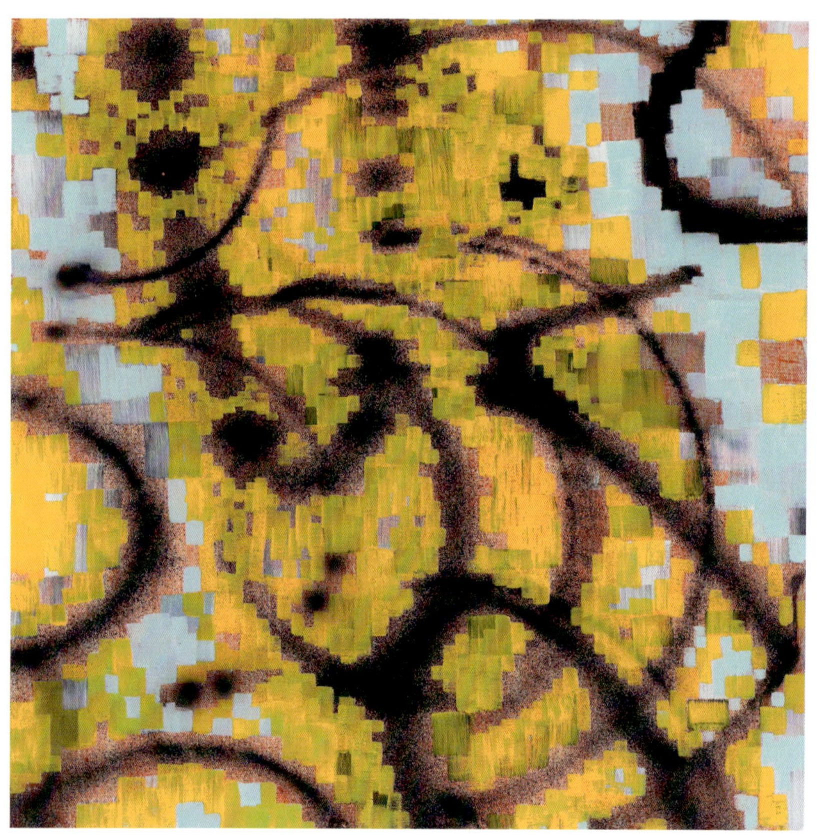

sexualities of the people who made them, but of course these have all affected my reading of their art. Artists who I suspect to be straight are included, but these are firmly in the minority. A bolder book might argue for the queerness of some of the lesbian imagery that male artists have produced. In an often formulaic field, cases can stand out – the artists appearing to access a rare cross-gender empathy – but they are not to be found here.

An art history that concentrates strictly on objects and the contexts of their reception misses important sides of the queer story. For this is, in part, a story of individual makers and of how they have grappled with the specific social pressures that apply to them. To pick up a paintbrush as a white, bisexual woman in 1920s Paris is different to pointing a video camera as a genderqueer, South Asian artist in Sydney today. And the reception of such artists' works will be markedly different. Those viewing art from any position of marginalised status can be acutely conscious of who made it. The opportunity to experience some degree of shared identity with the person behind an artwork can be an important source of pleasure for queer audiences. This was as true for Edwardian men who swooned over Michelangelo's buffed-up male nudes as for any queer teenager who skips a heartbeat at a surprise pronoun in a pop lyric. Works of art are gifts that sometimes help us to feel less out of place in the world. Alongside queer novels, films, poems and songs, art has played its part in nurturing the self-awareness and confidence of queer people around the world.

Today, it is the Internet that forms the most important conduit for the world's rapidly evolving queer cultures. Opening up global platforms for self-publication and reducing physical distance to a minor obstacle, the Internet has enabled far-flung

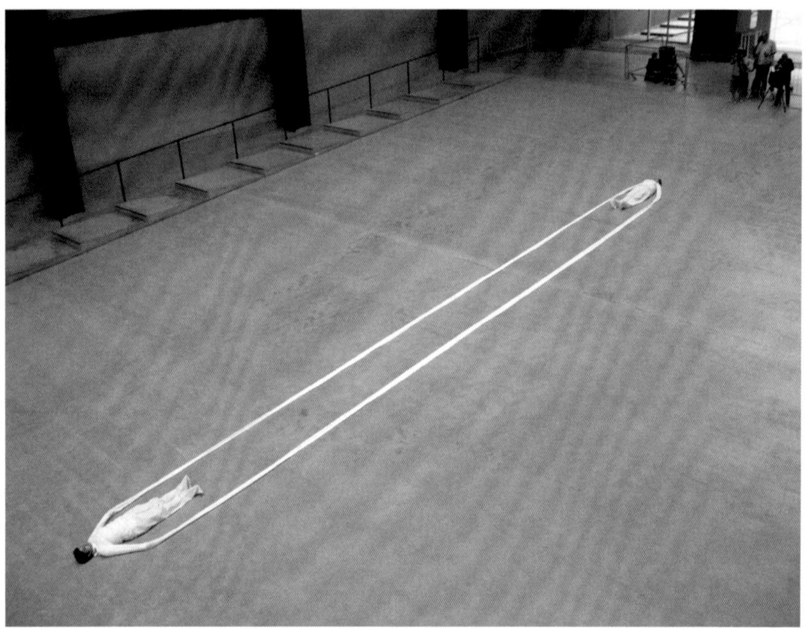

Tejal Shah
Encounter(s) VI 2006
Digital photograph on archival
rag paper
81.5 x 107
Photograph of live performance,
Turbine Hall, Tate Modern 2006,
in collaboration with Varsha Nair.

communities to develop around shared experiences or sensibilities. It has popularised new queer vocabulary and brought wider recognition to the variety of queer identities. In the process, it has sometimes sharpened divisions and intensified wounding conflicts beneath that queer umbrella. But at its most benign, the Internet helps erode the isolation of lives outside the norms. *Encounter(s)* was a 2006 performance by artists Tejal Shah (b.1979) and Varsha Nair (b.1957) staged at three venues, including London's Tate Modern (above).[3] The collaborators wore enveloping costumes of embroidered white fabric, joined by shared sleeves many metres long. Working far apart in Mumbai and Bangkok, Shah and Nair had come to know each other via email. *Encounter(s)* staged

the queer experience of online kinship: that feeling
of being more intimately connected to another
thousands of miles away than to the neighbours
in one's own street.

The Web is also coming to play more of a role in
linking up queer artists with appreciative audiences.
The career pathway now established in the offline art
world involves winning over a series of gatekeepers:
dealers, collectors, critics and curators. Many queer
artists have navigated this route with great success,
but other ways to build reputations are emerging.
The young, queer artist Mark Aguhar (1987–2012,
pp.138–9) acquired plenty of ardent admirers when
still a college student; her Tumblr blog had more far-
reaching influence than her exhibition CV. Aguhar's
all-too-brief career may be a foretaste of the range
of voices we will hear increasingly in years to come,
as queer and trans artists of colour find new ways to
overcome old obstacles.

Lastly, as I have come to appreciate through
working on this book, the Web now provides an
invaluable resource for anyone researching queer
art history. It accelerated the intensive process of
selecting these artworks and helped point me in
directions I might otherwise have missed. And yet,
despite their physical constraints, books have for
centuries been serving readers as highways into
queer territory. I hope this little book will do the same.

THE WORKS

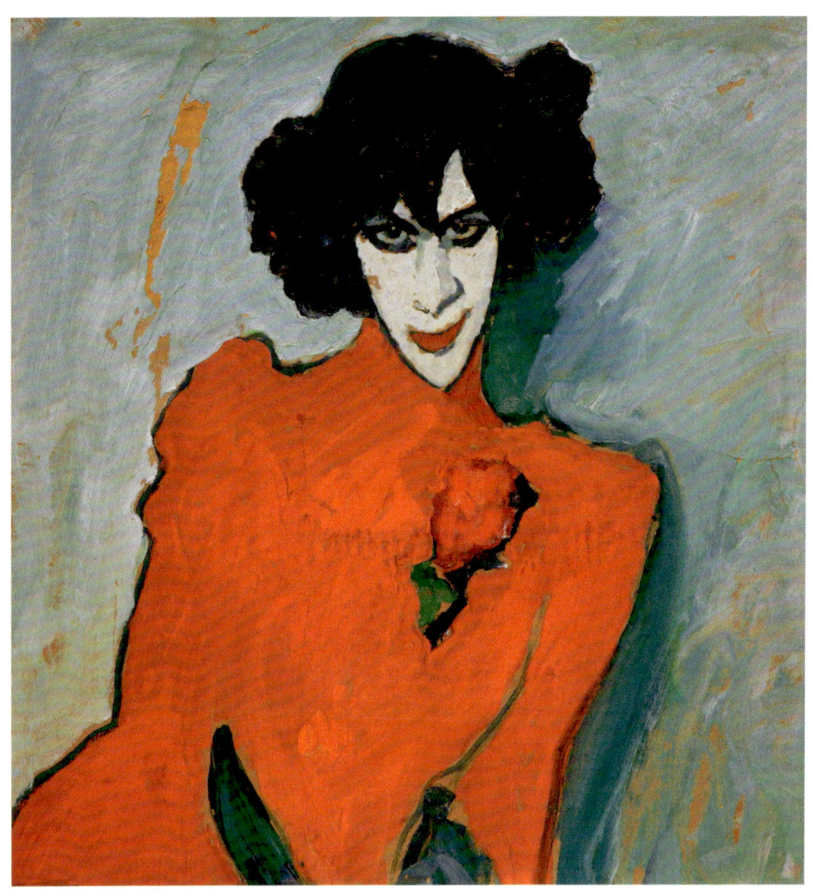

Alexej von Jawlensky
b.1864 Russia
d.1941 Germany
*Portrait of the Dancer
Alexander Sakharoff*

1909
Oil paint on cardboard
69.5 x 66.5
Städtische Galerie im
Lenbachhaus, Munich

This young, scarlet-clad Ukrainian dancer was part of the same avant-garde Munich set as Jawlensky, and was painted by the artist on several occasions. Perhaps the most engaging of those portraits, the painting was dashed off at speed when Sakharoff (1886–1963) happened to visit the artist's studio in costume, before a performance. It is said that Sakharoff grabbed the painting, still wet, from Jawlensky's easel, fearful lest the artist be tempted to paint over it. It remained in the dancer's possession for life.

It's easy to understand Sakharoff's determination to preserve this captivating image, which still routinely throws its viewers. For, in case you haven't yet spotted the twist, the sitter for this painting was male. Alexander Sakharoff's stage persona at this time represents a venture into genderqueer territory that would be seen as radical today, never mind in Wilhelmine Bavaria.

Sakharoff would go on to achieve international fame alongside Clotilde von Derp. The two dancers formed a lifelong partnership – both artistic and romantic. Rather sadly, the photos of Sakharoff from those later years never quite live up to the early images, as seen through Jawlensky's eyes. The luxurious locks were eventually cut back to a more masculine style, the make-up toned down and the costumes, which Sakharoff designed, became a little more conventional in terms of gender signals. Yet in this portrayal from the outset of Sakharoff's career, Jawlensky's glowing colours and fluid handling of paint seem to utterly dissolve the borderlines between genders.

Egon Schiele didn't go in for conventional self-portraits. Even to depict oneself naked was, in 1910, a bold artistic gesture with few precedents. The expressive distortions of the figure are entirely Schiele's own – born of weeks of intensely productive self-scrutiny before the mirror. A prodigy with an insatiable appetite for drawing, Schiele was not yet twenty when he created this portrait. His radical stylistic experiments were evolving almost month by month.

This drawing dates from the time of Schiele's friendship with fellow painter Max Oppenheimer (1885–1954). Older and already distorting his figures with expressive freedom, Oppenheimer probably nudged Schiele in new directions when the pair shared a Viennese studio in 1910. Oppenheimer was gay, while, as far as we know, Schiele's erotic activities were all heterosexual. After this crossing of paths, however, the younger artist would leave us with the queerer work. Even if you discount Schiele's many erotic drawings of paired women (typical male fantasies?) or his elfin male couples (narcissistic self-portraits?), there remain some of the most imaginatively sexed nudes in modern art.

Between those angular shoulders lie unmistakably rounded breasts. Follow the green belly, past the blue-black pubic hair, and you find genitals that blur distinctions between male and female. Throughout his many naked self-portraits, Schiele periodically reengineered his physical sex. He might exaggerate his penis to grandiose proportions or obliterate it entirely. The artist's freewheeling colour schemes often suggest a smattering of make-up on his own bony features.

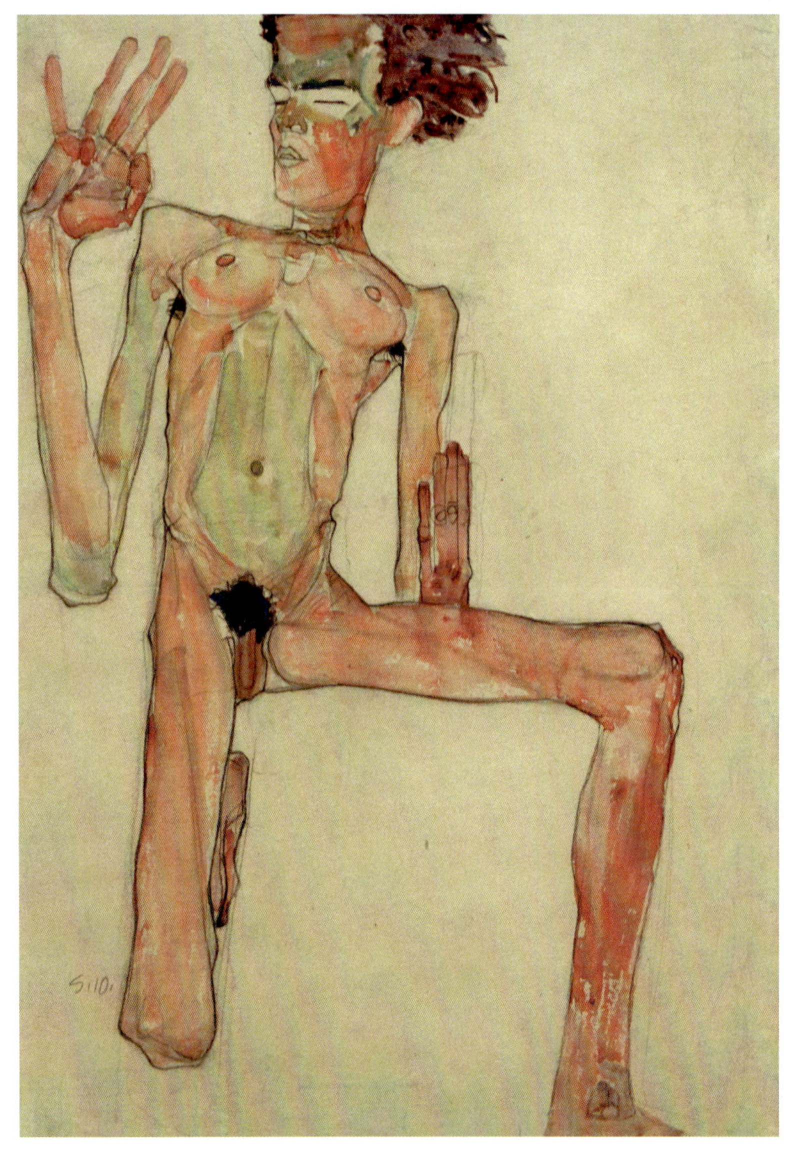

S.10.

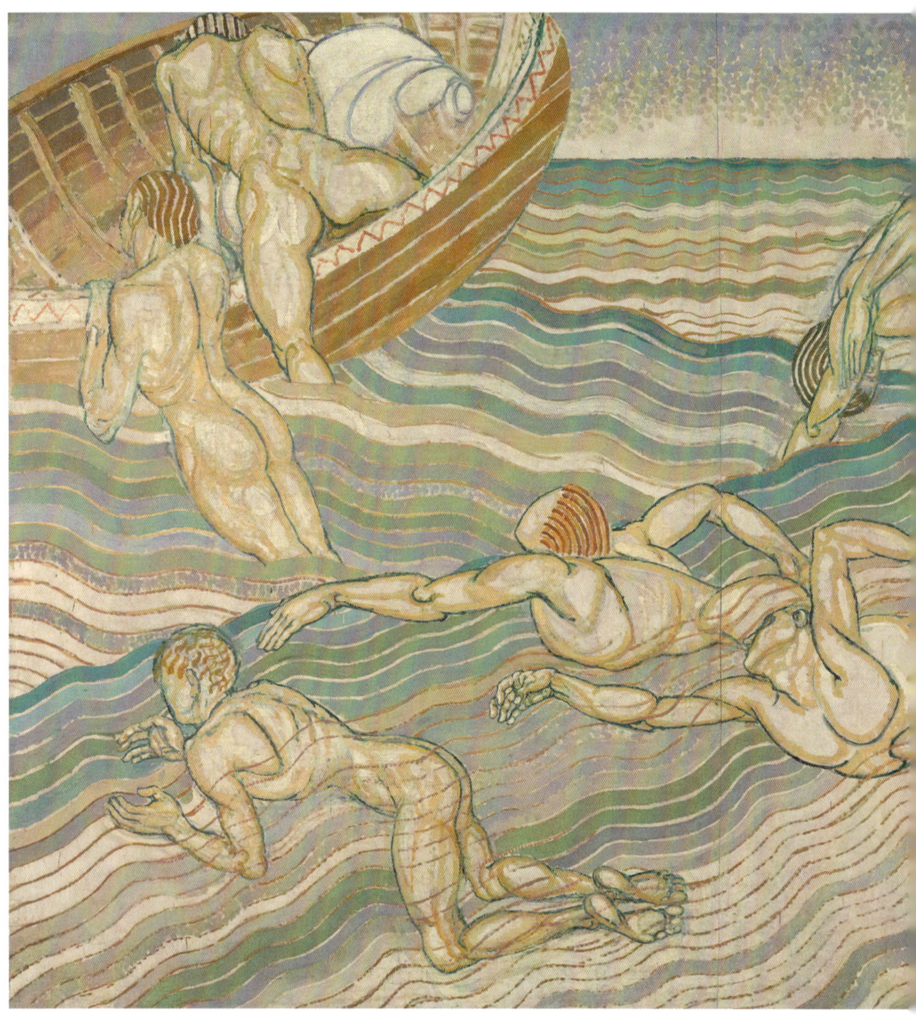

Duncan Grant

1885–1978 UK

Bathing

1911
Oil paint on canvas
228.6 × 306.1
Tate. Purchased 1931

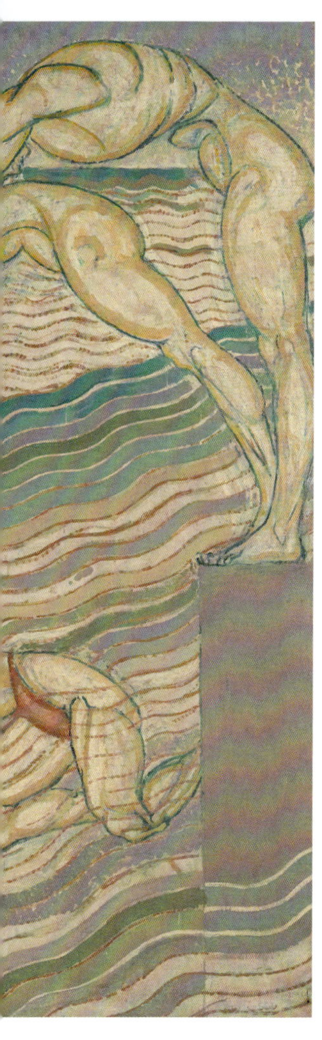

Bathing once formed part of a decorative scheme completed by six artists for a student dining hall at Borough Polytechnic, London. The overall theme was 'London on holiday'. Duncan Grant produced two of the seven murals and, while his colleagues all celebrated family-centred activities, his designs focus on athletic male bodies. In *Football*, he clearly enjoyed imagining skintight outfits to hug every bulging contour of his players. In *Bathing*, the clothes come off.

Nude outdoor bathing is now a Hollywood cliché for adolescent rebellion, but it was standard for men until the nineteenth century and survived well into the next. It inspired countless softly homoerotic scenes painted near the turn of the century across Europe and America; *Bathing* is one of the more stylistically adventurous examples. Hyde Park's Serpentine, the setting here, was a men-only swimming spot until the 1930s and nude bathing was still common then. Naked men brought admirers. The Serpentine was on the unofficial gay sightseeing list, even if park regulations attempted to bar voyeurs from the lido.[4]

Adept at picking up male lovers, Grant understood the gay viewpoint he was implicitly presenting. He underlines his message with a set of poses that are almost scandalously suggestive. (Imagine the water gone for a moment!) For good measure, he throws in a nude whose pose – as cultured queer observers would have spotted – quotes a work by Michelangelo: the favoured Renaissance ancestor figure for gay male artists.[5] Perhaps it's no surprise that one Edwardian hack, writing in the *National Review*, condemned the corrupting influence the dining hall murals would have on young students.[6]

Roberto Montenegro
1885–1968 Mexico
*Vaslav Nijinsky as
Daphnis in Mikhail
Fokine's ballet
Daphnis and Chloe*

1912, printed 1913
Print with gold highlighting
on art board
31.5 x 23.9
Victoria and Albert Museum,
London

In the story of modern dance, the short-lived career of Vaslav Nijinsky (1889–1950) has assumed mythic stature. International audiences marvelled at the dancer's youthful athleticism, exhibited through five seasons with the Ballets Russes. In his dazzling *grand jeté* to stardom, Nijinsky became an erotic idol to fans of all genders, helped by stage costumes that were daringly revealing and frequently feminising. No wonder rock star David Bowie described his 1970s Ziggy Stardust persona as 'a cross between Nijinsky and Woolworths'.[7]

Bowie ascended to queer icon status in January 1972, when he told *Melody Maker* he was gay. If such a public acknowledgement was unthinkable in his day, it's still likely that Nijinsky's queer aura gained from rumours of his six-year relationship with Sergei Diaghilev (1872–1929) – founder of the Ballets Russes. It's telling how many queer artists drew, painted, sculpted or photographed the dancer at the height of his fame; besides Roberto Montenegro, the list includes John Singer Sargent (1856–1925), Glyn Philpot (pp.44–5), Jean Cocteau (1889–1963), Una Troubridge (1887–1963), George Barbier (1882–1932), Ethel Walker (pp.38–9) and Adolph de Meyer (1868–1946). Portraits doubled as fan merchandise. This example comes from a limited edition set printed from Montenegro's ink drawings, illustrating ten Nijinsky roles.[8]

Montenegro spent fourteen years in Europe before returning to become a leading figure in Mexican mural painting. Like Diaghilev, the young artist fell under the queer spell of 1890s illustrator Aubrey Beardsley (1872–98). In this image, emulating Beardsley's stylised outlines, Nijinsky's body is strangely extended and fetishised. The dancer's compact head and thick, curving neck seem almost as phallic as the cylindrical rose tree, while the skimpy tunic teases us by nearly revealing the mystery sex of this androgynous figure.

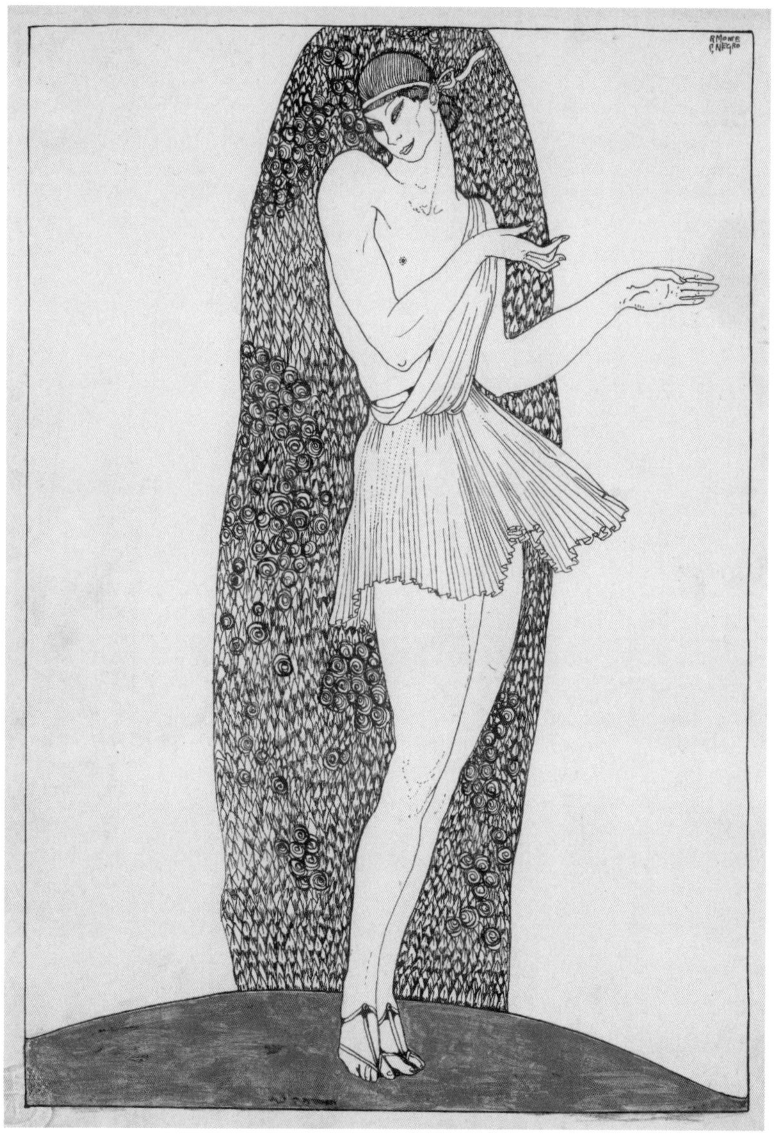
R MONTE
C. NEGRO

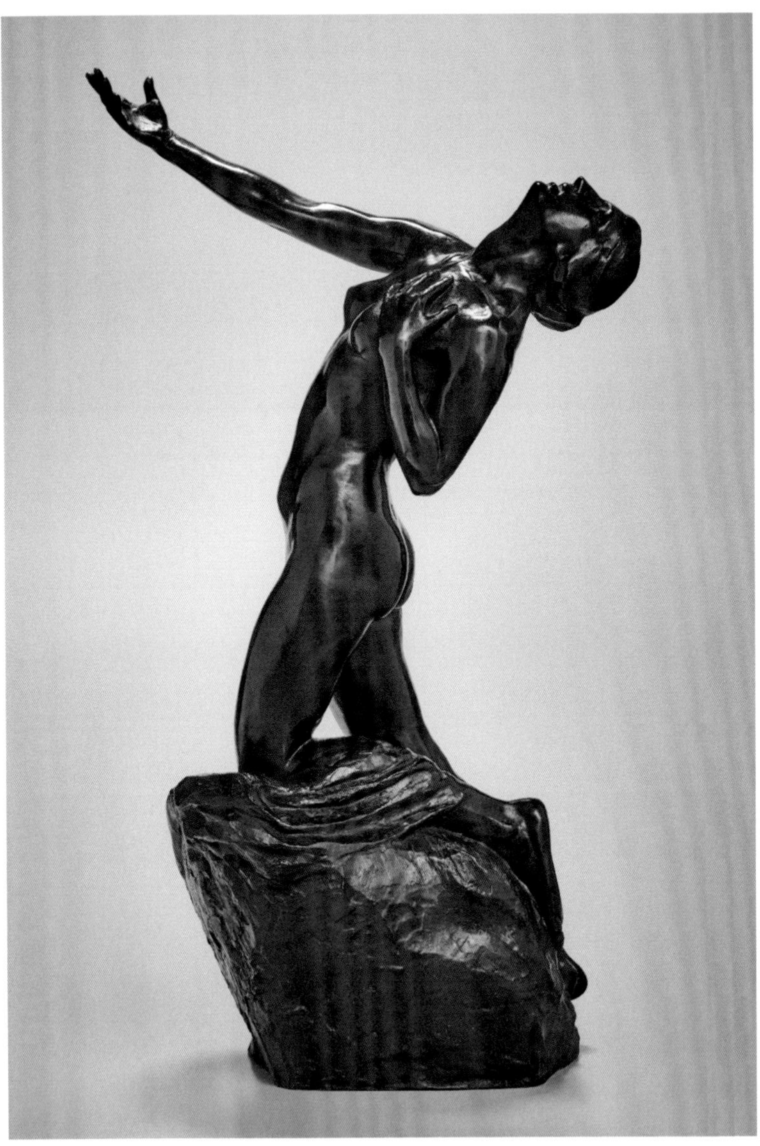

Florence Wyle

b.1881 USA
d.1968 Canada
Sun Worshipper

c.1916
Bronze
67.6 x 23.9 x 33.2
National Gallery of Canada,
Ottawa

Florence Wyle was a quiet rebel who shook off the dust of a conservative rural Illinois upbringing to pursue a bohemian life in a new country. At twenty-one, after three years of university medical studies, Wyle realised her true calling and headed north to train at the Art Institute of Chicago. It was there, two years later, that she met Frances Loring (1887–1968). Soon inseparable, the two sculptors shared a home and studio over the course of almost sixty years. A whirl in New York's Greenwich Village was followed in 1913 by a permament move to Canada. In Toronto, the pair resided in a ramshackle old church, becoming known locally as the Loring-Wyles, or simply as The Girls.

Wyle sculpted the female body throughout her career, combining an appreciation for naked beauty with a solid understanding of naturalistic anatomy. Imbued with a sense of drama that defies its modest size, *Sun Worshipper* is a free-spirited statement from Wyle's first years in Toronto. It was purchased in 1918 for the National Gallery: a measure of the splash that these US-trained arrivals made in Canada's relatively small pond of sculptors. The work's title and rocky base imply the young woman is exposing all to the sky. Nudism (or naturism) was a modish pastime in the early decades of the century, although it was only just beginning to hit Canadian shores; Wyle's *Sun Worshipper* actually anticipates the country's first naturist club by a couple of years. Basking in the rays, she arches her supple body in a show of unabashed ecstasy that hints more than a little at sexual pleasures.

GAN (Gösta Adrian-Nilsson)

1884–1965 Sweden
Sailors and Panthers

1917
Oil paint on canvas
95 × 95
Private collection

Sailors have traditionally attracted queer admirers. Fetching uniforms aside, the seafaring life was widely believed to instil a flexible attitude towards whatever sexual opportunities might arise. For much of the twentieth century, when gay nightspots were uncommon at best, bars or open spaces near docks represented a worthwhile bet for those seeking sex with other men. Gösta Adrian-Nilsson – known simply as 'GAN' – often spent nights on the prowl after moving to Stockholm in 1916, much like the cats that sniff around in his painting *Sailors and Panthers*. Besides being an erotic fixation, sailors began to dominate his art. In 1918, he mounted a whole exhibition titled *Sailor Compositions*.

GAN started taking his art in radical modernist directions in his thirties, following exposure to avant-grade influences in Berlin. *Sailors and Panthers* demonstrates his quest to create a fusion of expressionist, cubist and futurist painting styles. If read as an exercise in futurist 'dynamism' – a means of evoking motion through repeated, broken outlines – the painting could be understood as one seaman tracked by a lone, predatory panther (perhaps a metaphorical self-portrait). More likely, the pack of three panthers act as doubles of the sailor trio – their identity implied through matching head turns. To seek nocturnal companions among working men on the street in GAN's day was to risk blackmail or violence. GAN's imagery, unveiling the danger behind the sailors' sexual appeal in the shape of deadly felines, may echo a queer literary source. In *De Profundis*, the imprisoned Oscar Wilde (1854–1900) – an author GAN idolised to the point of imitation – recollects consorting with 'trade' as 'like feasting with panthers; the danger was half the excitement'.[9]

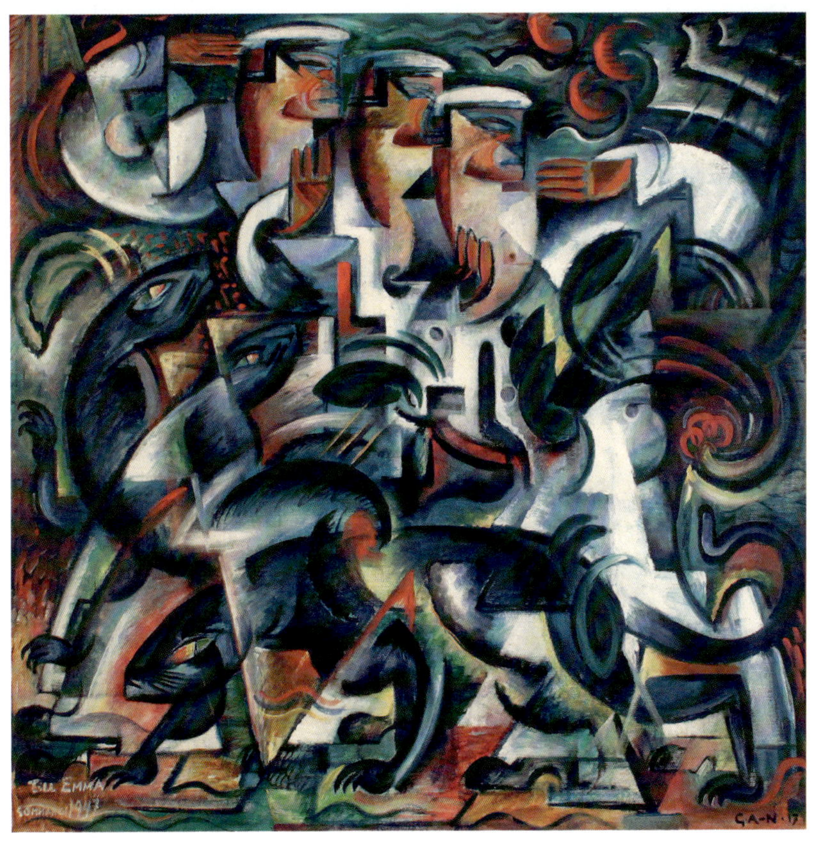

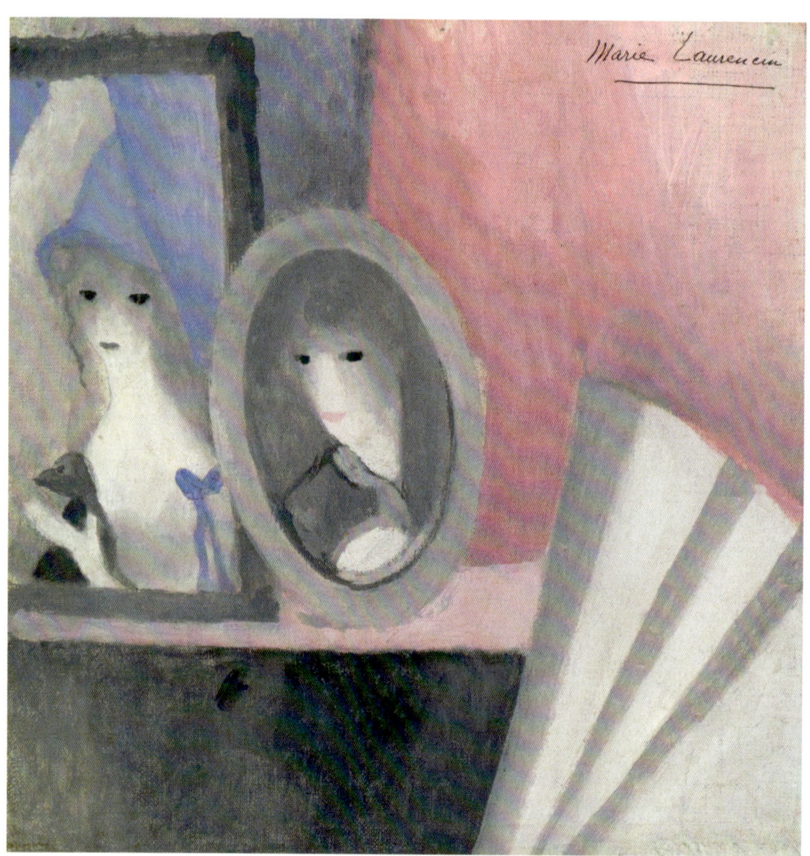

Marie Laurencin

1885–1956 France
The Fan
L'Eventail

c.1919
Oil paint on canvas
30.5 x 30
Tate. Bequeathed by
Elly Kahnweiler 1991,
accessioned 1994

Marie Laurencin has received a bumpy ride from art history. Before turning thirty, she stood out – briefly – as perhaps the most modern woman artist in France; her associates ranged from Pablo Picasso to Gertrude Stein. After her death, she sank into obscurity for decades, until a conjunction of Japanese collectors and feminist art historians began a reappraisal that is ongoing. As a result, the queer dimensions of Laurencin's life and art are at last attracting detailed scrutiny.

Laurencin had relationships with both men and women but, in her art, preferred to imagine a world peopled almost exclusively with female friends and lovers. Her dreamy, pastel-hued paintings have been too easy to class as unchallenging versions of femininity. On close inspection, her balletic wraiths and sidesaddle Amazons, dressed in wisps of muted pink and cornflower blue, are clearly into each other. This is queer femme with a Gallic twist.

The pairing of framed images in *The Fan* is a pictorial puzzle that hints at same-sex romance. The face in the oval frame is recognisable – albeit thanks to other self-portraits – as Laurencin herself. This implies that we look through the artist's eyes at a mirror, and the raised left hand we see in our/Laurencin's reflection surely holds the fan that dominates the foreground. The status of the woman within the rectangular frame is less clear: is she a picture, or a reflection in a second mirror at a slightly different angle? The first option might suggest Laurencin's thoughts of an absent lover; the second would place the two women in the same intimate space (perhaps a bedroom).

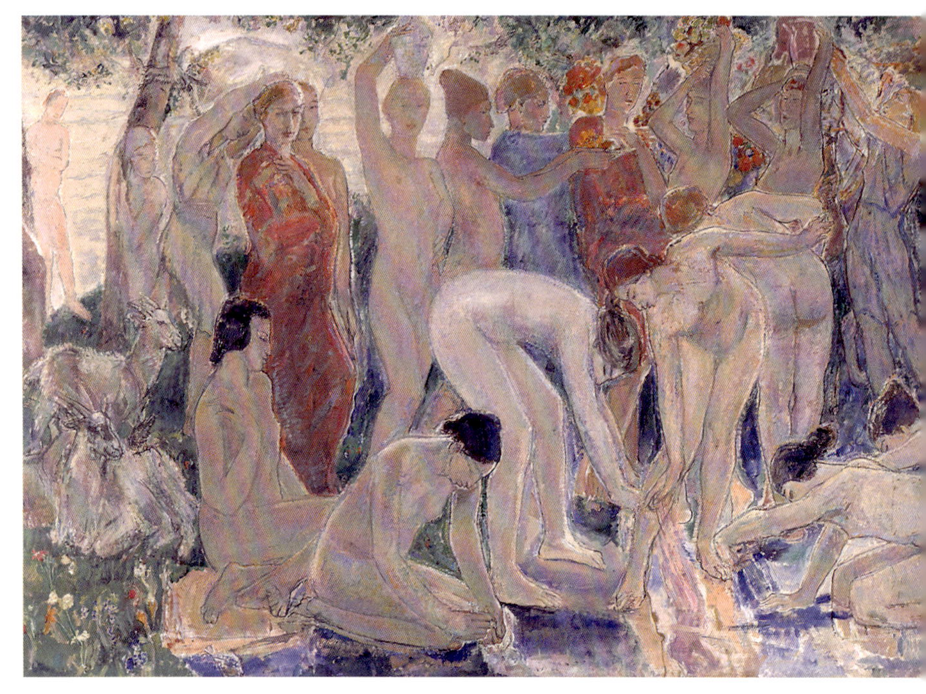

Dame Ethel Walker

1861–1951 UK

Decoration:
The Excursion of Nausicaa

1920
Oil paint on canvas
183.5 × 367
Tate. Purchased 1924

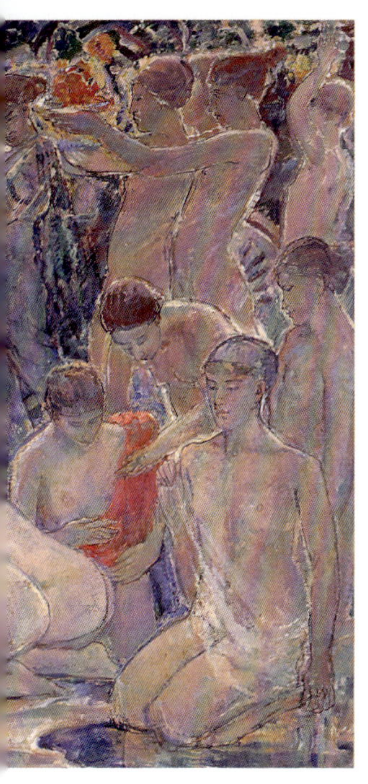

In Ethel Walker's *Excursion of Nausicaa*, the young Phaeacian princess, a key character in *The Odyssey*, has led her retinue of maidens down to the river estuary to wash the palace laundry. They make a fun day of it by bringing a royal picnic and taking a bathe – followed by an olive oil rub-down and some Bronze-Age ball games. It's at this point that they disturb the shipwrecked Odysseus, who has been sleeping in the woods near the shore. Nausicaa comes to the aid of the hungry and naked Greek hero, but if you're expecting heterosexual romance to blossom, you'll be disappointed (perhaps like Odysseus himself).

Previous paintings of this tale from Homer traditionally made Odysseus the focal point. But if he features at all in Walker's version, it must be as the faint and oddly boyish figure at the left edge, deep in the background. This lesbian artist has created a version of the story that is unquestionably woman-centred, gently homoerotic, and on an impressively grand scale. Six-feet high and almost twelve across, this probably set a new record for the biggest Sapphic beach party in Western art.

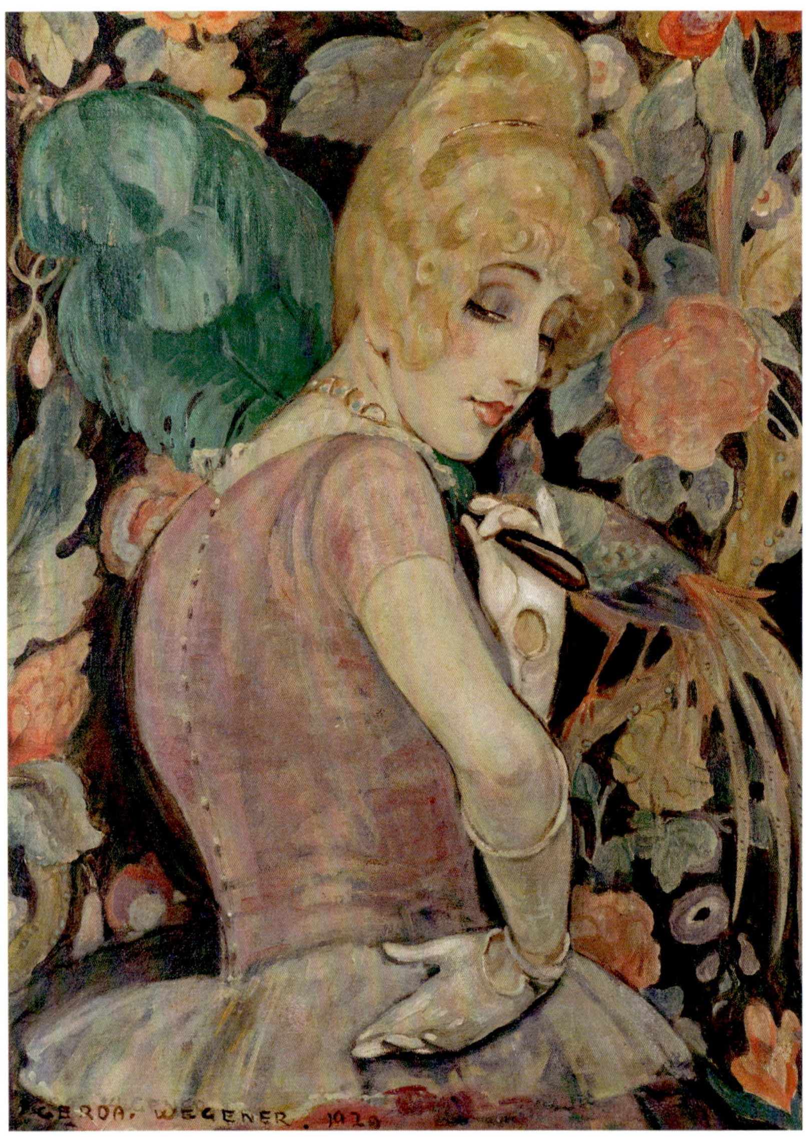

Gerda Wegener
1885–1940 Denmark
Lili With a Feather Fan

1920
Oil paint on canvas
79 x 59
Private collection

When nineteen-year-old Gerda Gottlieb married a fellow painter named Einar Wegener in 1904, she cannot have imagined the fascination their marriage would stir among future novelists, academics and film-makers. It would prove an affectionate and trusting partnership; and yet, in 1931, the Wegener marriage was deemed impossible and dissolved by royal decree. The circumstances were unprecedented. Gerda's spouse was now Lili Ilse Elvenes – her new chosen name – though she is better known to us today as Lili Elbe, the name used in media reports of her pioneering gender transition.

Long before Lili burst into the daylight following her now famous series of surgeries, she lived and breathed in Gerda's paintings. In private, Lili became Gerda's favourite model: sometimes dressed in the chic fashions of their adopted Paris; other times nude; always doe-eyed and cherry-lipped. Via her celebratory paintings – such as *Lili With a Feather Fan* – Gerda displayed a remarkable will to honour her partner's emerging identity as a fully realised truth.

Gerda's paintings of Lili were popular at the time and have fuelled a current revival of interest in the artist. Yet there is much more to Wegener's career as a painter, cartoonist and hotly in-demand illustrator of the art deco era. Some of her watercolours of fashionable Parisian social life feature scenes of lesbian flirtation. Her most erotic book illustrations, too risqué to sign with her name, depict sex between women. It's an artistic legacy that suggests Gerda Wegener challenged sexual norms along with embracing Lili's challenge to gender norms.

Carl Milles
1875–1955 Sweden
The Sun Singer (Torso)

1922
Bronze
91.1 x 29.2 x 24.1
Tate. Bequeathed by
Mrs Muriel Elverston 1977

The Swedish Academy of Letters commissioned a monument to national poet Esaias Tegnér (1782–1846) from Carl Milles in 1918, expecting a portrait. The sculptor instead drew inspiration from a revered Tegnér lyric, *Song to the Sun*, and delivered a twelve-foot Apollonian male nude who sings to this day from the Stockholm waterfront, bronze arms outstretched to the wind.

Minus arms and head, this smaller sculpture otherwise resembles its giant cousin. Its streamlined, muscular physique is typical of Milles' male nudes, which account for a major chunk of his output. Whatever the sculptor's motivations (he was married to a woman), these works have attracted gay fans ever since they were first unveiled. One such fan was American banking heir and art collector Robert Allerton. Entranced by a 1927 exhibition of Milles' work at the Tate Gallery, Allerton went on to commission a full-size cast of *The Sun Singer* for his private sculpture garden at Monticello, Illinois. Most of us make do with postcards.

What was it about sun worship a century ago? The parade of homoerotic naturists in early twentieth-century art extends beyond the examples in this book by Milles and Florence Wyle (see pp.32–3). An earlier bronze figure by the gay German sculptor Sascha Schneider (*Sun Worshipper* c.1912, Schloss Eckberg, Dresden) and a nude youth in a woodland landscape by English painter Henry Scott Tuke (*To the Morning Sun* 1903, Hugh Lane Gallery, Dublin) strike similar poses to *The Sun Singer*. All this outdoor exhibitionism may be a form of closeted gay code. Apollo/Helios, the eternally youthful sun god of the Greeks, was a long-established focus for queer male desire.

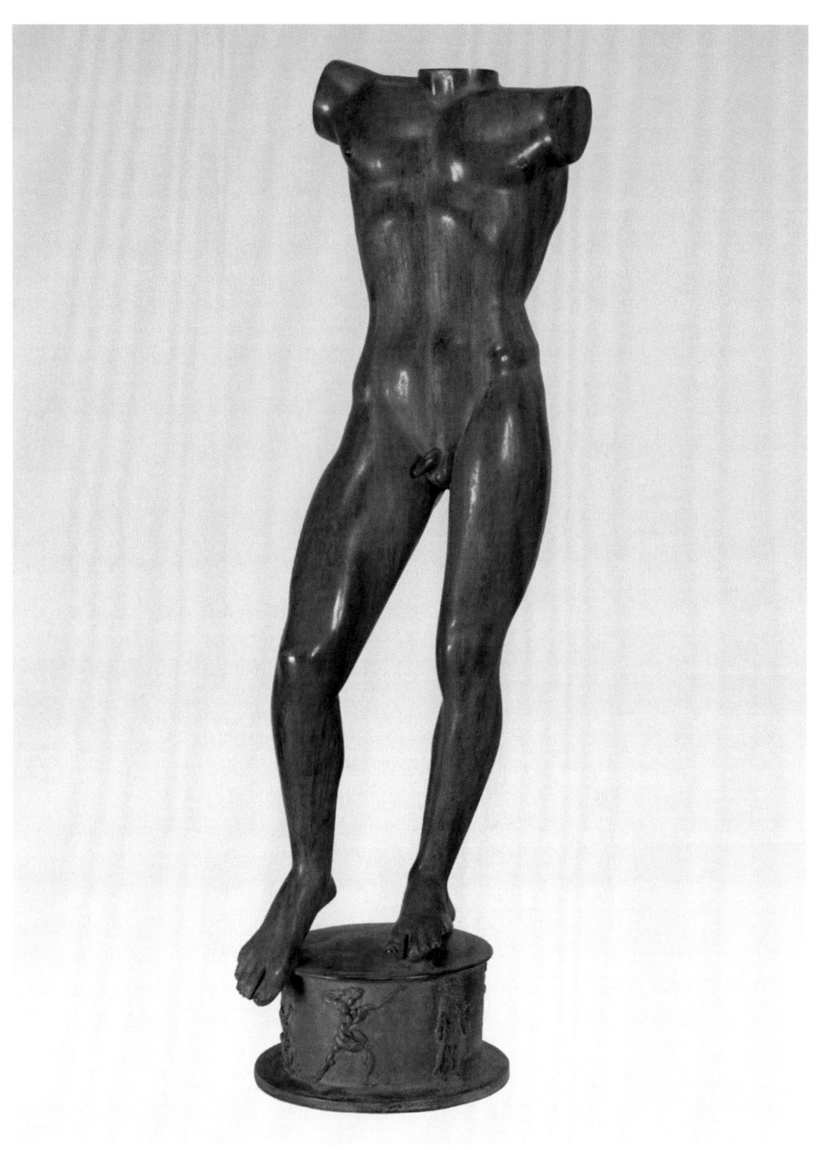

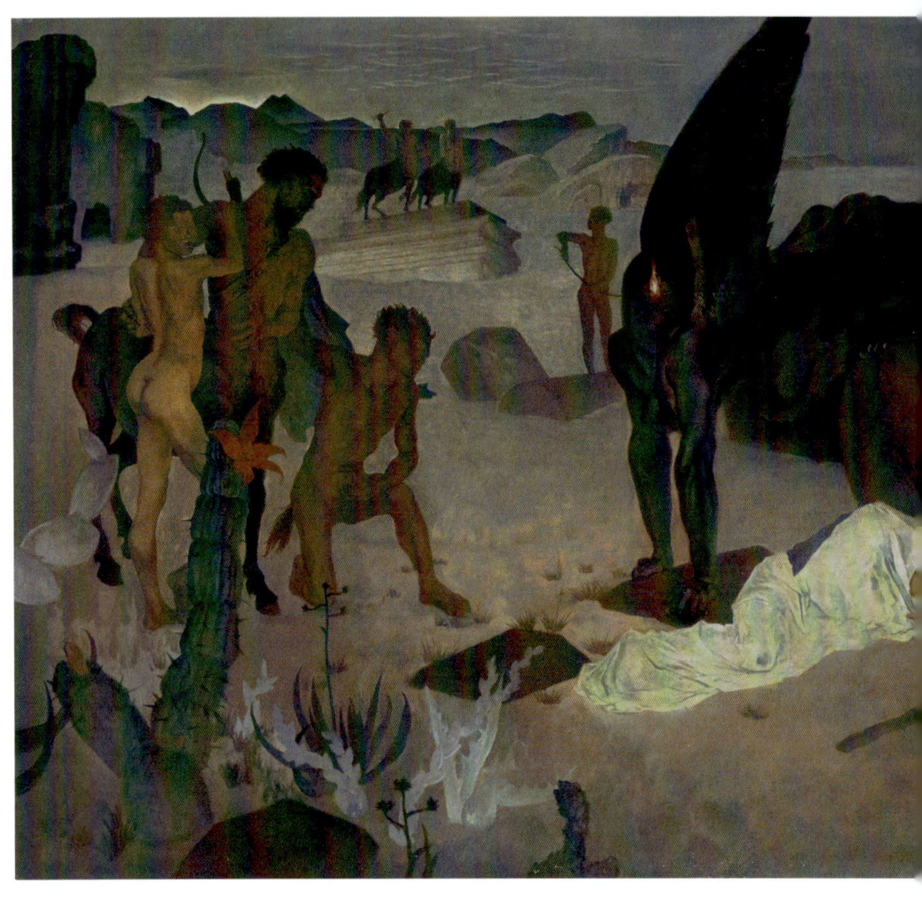

Glyn Warren Philpot

1884–1937 UK

*Repose on the
Flight into Egypt*

1922
Oil paint on canvas
74.9 x 116.1
Tate. Purchased 2004

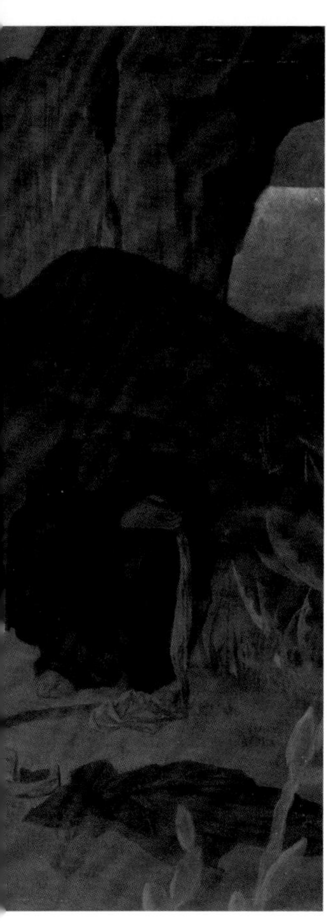

Glyn Philpot struggled to shake off his early typecasting as a painter of flattering society portraits. *Repose on the Flight into Egypt* is arguably the best of several idiosyncratic ventures into religious territory. Journeying into exile to evade Herod's assassins, the Holy Family huddle for shelter by a colossal fallen statue. A curious sphinx, fauns and centaurs – mythical creatures associated with the pre-Christian Mediterranean world – have quietly assembled to witness the newly arrived Christ. The mysterious image might almost be titled 'The Adoration of the Monsters'.

Hybrid creatures often stalk the realms of queer imagination. Philpot's mentor Charles Ricketts (1866–1931) illustrated a lavish edition of Oscar Wilde's coded, erotic poem *The Sphinx*. Vaslav Nijinsky became a queer icon through his performance as a faun (see also pp.30–1). Centaurs and minotaurs still crop up both in gay erotic comics and in queer contemporary art.[10] Such creatures of the wilds embody the promise of sensuality untrammelled by human social conventions.

During the Italian Renaissance of the fifteenth century, these sexy, classically-inspired hybrids returned to the stage of Western art, coinciding with a rediscovery of the idealised male nude. Many gay aesthetes – including Wilde, Ricketts and Philpot – felt strong affinities for Renaissance art, and *Repose on the Flight into Egypt* was actually painted in Florence, cradle of the style. During his Italian stay, Philpot made sure to visit Orvieto Cathedral, where an impressive parade of nudes in frescoes by Luca Signorelli (c.1440/50–1523) are ever popular with gay tourists. A figure borrowed from Signorelli can be found in the polyamorous queer triad at the left of this painting (directly behind a stridently phallic cactus).[11]

Romaine Brooks

b.1874 Italy
d.1970 France
*Peter (A Young
English Girl)*

1923–4
Oil paint on canvas
91.9 x 62.3
Smithsonian American
Art Museum, Washington DC

'The all-time ultimate gallery of all the famous dykes from 1889 to 1935 or thereabouts.' That's how Truman Capote (1924–84) recalled the contents of Romaine Brooks' studio, which he visited in Paris as a young man.[12] The writer's personal guide to this treasure trove was Natalie Barney (1876–1972): Brooks' lover and still, in her 70s, the city's reigning lesbian hostess. Capote was fifty years younger than these wealthy American expatriates, and so struck by the couple's impressive roster of queer cultural connections he even pushed the reach of Brooks' output backwards by around twenty years. The extraordinary run of images Brooks painted from 1910 to around 1925 continues to impress. Hers is one of the earliest sustained commitments to queer art making.

One of the most alluring of the whole bunch is this portrait of rakishly beautiful British artist, Gluck (1895–1978). Depending on your reading of Gluck's transgressive masculine persona, the painting and its riddling title either open or close down radical possibilities for queer genders. Does the 'girl' of Brooks' title establish a subversive space for a modern, androgynous mode of femininity, or force a prescriptive gender label on to an individual at pains to reject such signifiers? Part of the appeal of the term 'queer' as a tool for reading art from this period is that it permits such questions to remain without a definitive answer. Only in recent decades has a neat distinction been made between the axes of sexuality and gender identity. To claim Gluck as categorically either a lesbian or a transmasculine artist is to project our own models of identity back in time.

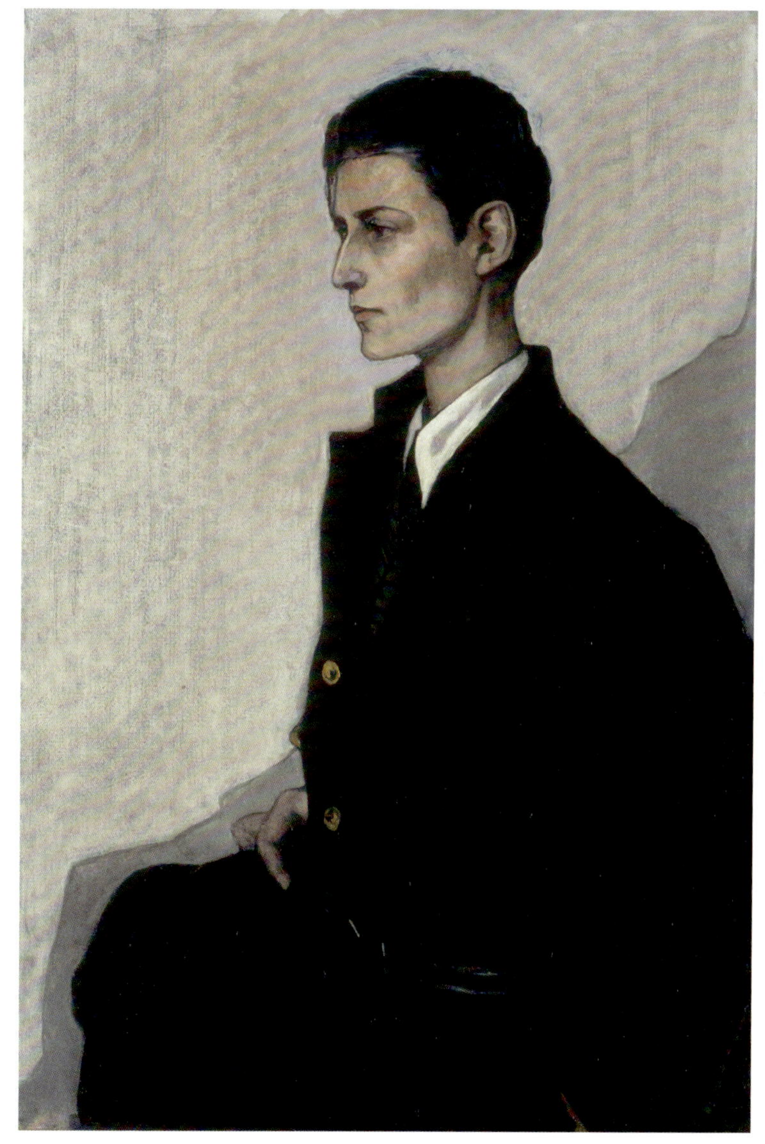

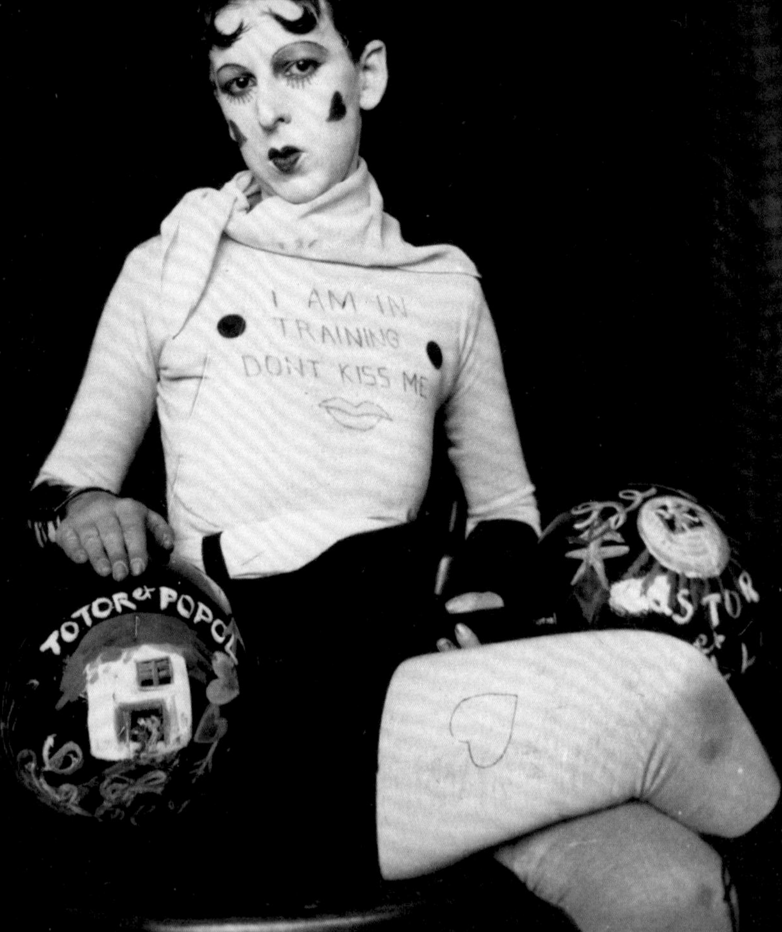
I AM IN
TRAINING
DONT KISS ME
TOTOR et POPOL
CASTOR

Claude Cahun
b.1894 France
d.1954 Jersey
Self Portrait

1927
Photograph on paper
11.7 x 8.9
Jersey Heritage Trust

Almost four decades after Claude Cahun died in obscurity on the island of Jersey, this writer, artist and anti-Nazi resistance activist returned from the grave. In the early 1990s, a cluster of books, articles and exhibitions revealed Cahun's previously unknown photographic legacy. A generation schooled in queer and postmodernist thought rushed to embrace the forgotten artist as a prophet. Though Cahun's literary works and surrealist constructions are impressive, the artist's cult following is a response to the extraordinary self-portraits, in which genders are swapped and mixed. This 'weightlifter' photograph has become one of the most revered (and regularly impersonated) queer icons of the twentieth century.

A circus costume with appliqué nipples sheaths Cahun's presumably bound chest (breasts are in evidence in other photographs). The emblazoned message pleads, 'I AM IN TRAINING DONT KISS ME.' Despite the strongman outfit, the persona is among the least butch to be found among Cahun's surviving photographs. Hair that was sometimes shaved or severely cropped is here shaped into kiss-curls. The artist has engineered a gender-confounding, 'sissy'-drag ensemble, rounded off with love hearts and a face painted like a doll.

Gender that strays beyond the female/male binary is a thread that runs through this artist's life and work. It starts with the adopted, unisex name Claude (Cahun was born Lucy Schwob) and its apex is found in *Disavowals*: Cahun's major literary work (published 1930). 'Masculine? Feminine? It depends on the situation. Neuter is the only gender that always suits me.'[13] Though this surrealist text is no more trustworthy a portrait of its author than the carefully staged photographs, Cahun still offers our own age a foretaste of queer negotiations with the gender binary.

Edward Burra
1905–76 UK
The Snack Bar

1930
Oil paint on canvas
76.2 x 55.9
Tate. Purchased 1980

Whatever city this is, *The Snack Bar* must operate in one of its livelier *quartiers*. A lone woman in hat, coat and heavy make-up – possibly a resting sex worker – eats at a nocturnal counter, while a colleague loiters on the pavement outside. A saucy barman makes a great performance out of slicing an obscenely oversized salami, coordinating beautifully with his pink shirt. His eyebrows are pencilled in; spider lashes suggest a heavy dose of mascara; and that white eyeball, glancing sidelong at his customer, is ringed with a hint of blue eye-shadow.

A pair of male customers occupy the rear of the café. One – with a dove grey hat and another splash of eye make-up – is all but hidden by the woman in the foreground. Is he also plying his trade here? Or did these men hook up in a nearby bar before stopping here for a sandwich? His bespectacled companion stretches a hungry mouth wide to receive a finger-like morsel in what could easily be a visual pun on fellatio.

Edward Burra spent much of his life in the Sussex town of Rye in domestic seclusion, but his distinctive pictorial imagination feasted on city pleasures sampled during adventures in London or abroad. Though his sombre landscapes and sinister war allegories are also rightly celebrated, the artist is surely at his most 'Burraesque' in his urban scenes of the 1920s and 30s, populated by louche sailors and women in drag-style make-up. Like Burra's famously gossipy correspondence, these queer vignettes delight in innuendo and fizz with a generous measure of camp as acid as their colour palette.

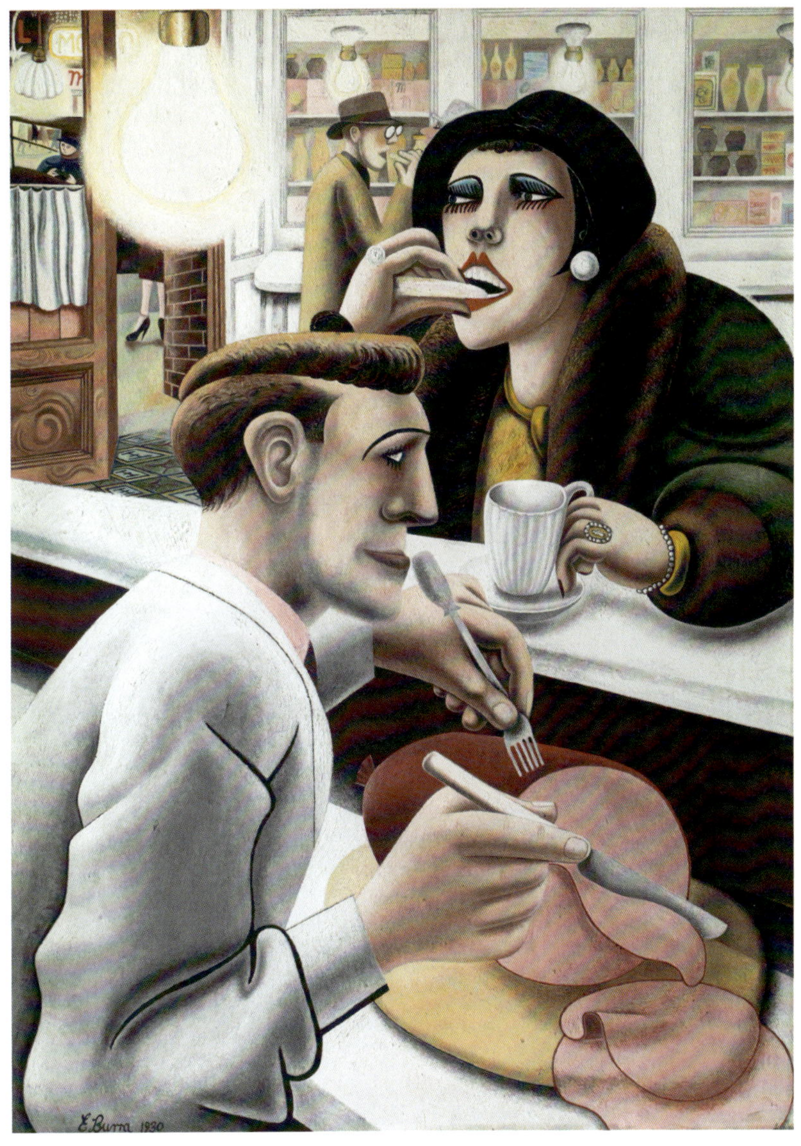

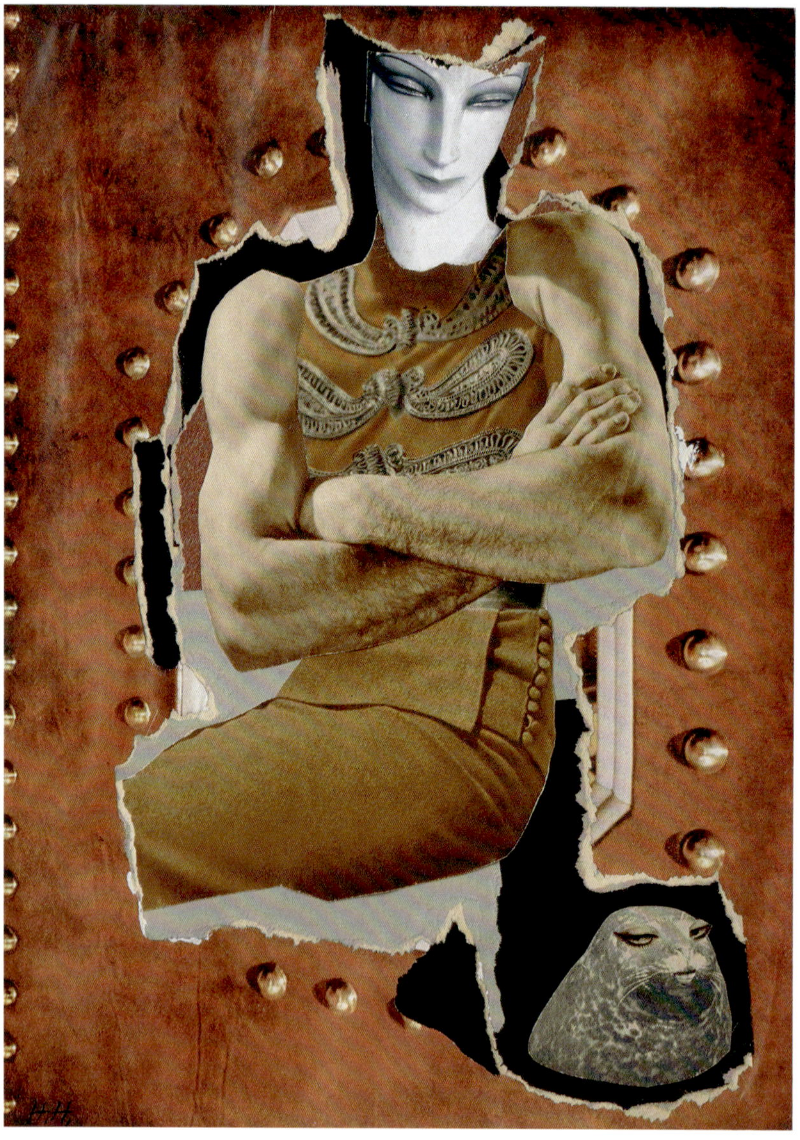

Hannah Höch

1889–1978 Germany
Dompteuse

c.1930, reworked 1963–4
Photomontage with
collage elements
35.5 x 26
Kunsthaus Zürich

In 1929, Hannah Höch held her first solo exhibition in The Hague, where she had moved three years earlier to be with Dutch writer Til Brugman (1888–1958). In the catalogue, she announced her artistic credo: 'I would like to blur the firm borders that we human beings, cocksure as we are, are inclined to erect around everything that is accessible to us.'[14]

From her days as the sole woman artist in Berlin's subversive dada group, Höch excelled at photomontage. Her early recombinations of images tend to be jarring and satirically grotesque, but the promise of that 1929 statement would be fulfilled with *Dompteuse*. Here, feminine and masculine elements merge in a seductive and strangely plausible synthesis: dominatrix-cum-butch-daddy. (Höch's French title means 'tamer'; the braided vest and seal underline the circus reference, but the word can also describe the dominant role in sexualised power play.) The artist's ten-year relationship with Brugman perhaps roused her to visualise queer genders and sexualities. These happened to be topics of intense, public scrutiny in Weimar Berlin, to where the couple returned in 1929. *Dompteuse* may even respond to debates around androgyny within contemporary German sexology.

With this image, Höch has swept away the 'firm border' of gender, rendering any attraction we experience towards the tamer decidedly queer; recognised hetero- and homosexual dynamics cease to apply.[15] I like to believe that Höch's own commentary on *Dompteuse* can be gathered from the concluding words of her Hague manifesto: 'I should like to make what seems impossible appear possible; I should like to help people to experience a richer world so that they may feel more kindly towards the world we know.'

Toyen
b.1902 Czech Republic
d.1980 France
Early Morning

1931
Oil paint on canvas
89 x 116
Moravian Gallery, Brno

I have become fascinated by the life and work of Toyen: queer anarcho-communist and founding member of the Surrealist Group of Czechoslovakia. What does that say about me? If I were writing in Czech, where verbs and adjectives have feminine and masculine inflections, that opening sentence might have already indicated my gender. And that is why Toyen intrigues; though given a female name at birth, the artist rejected female word forms and instead applied masculine alternatives. The adoption of the ungendered name 'Toyen' and the shifting gender styles of the artist's outfits add to the impression of one who lived at some distance from the female gender they were assigned.

Toyen's art is peppered with references to queer sexuality. It's quite a contrast to the serene abstraction of Marlow Moss (pp.66–7), Toyen's peer in the arena of gender non-conformity. Suggestions of female body parts are woven into Toyen's paintings, sometimes transposed on to unfamiliar objects in true surrealist fashion. More explicit are Toyen's erotic illustrations on heterosexual, lesbian or masturbatory themes, many published in the 1930s by close artistic comrade Jindrich Štyrský (1899–1942). In one striking drawing for Štyrský's *Erotická revue*, a naked figure composed of statue fragments – female above the hips and male below – reclines on a beach.[16] The fingers of Toyen's androgyne slip between large, vulva-like lips atop a hairy, rotund sea creature. In *Early Morning*, painted the previous year, colourful marine forms display similar labial clefts. It's one of a group of paintings exploring queer watery environments made throughout 1931, as Toyen transitioned from their richly-textured abstract work of the late 1920s to the fully-fledged surrealism of the 1930s.

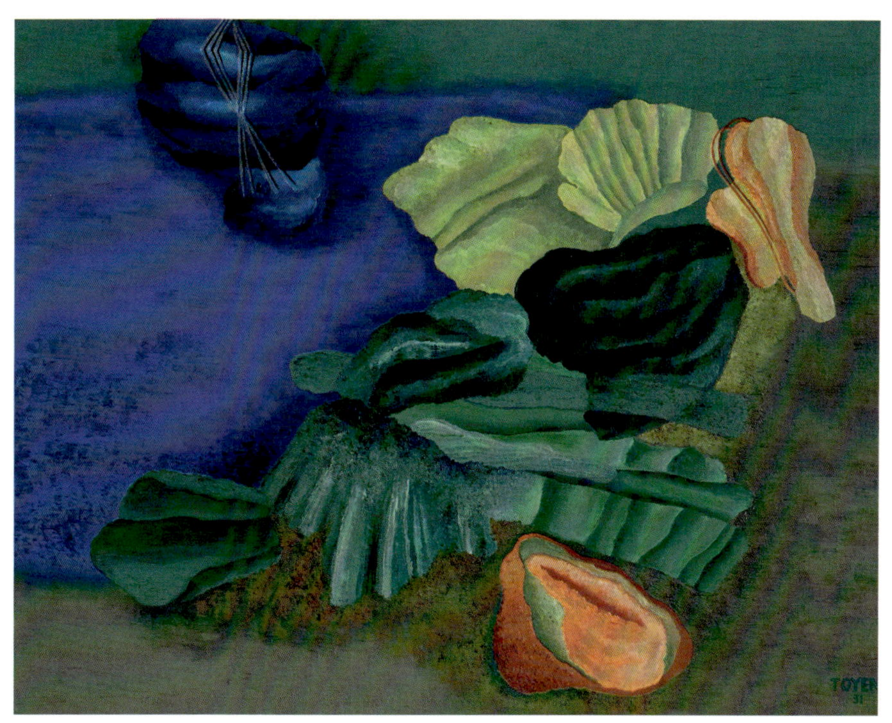

TOYEN
31

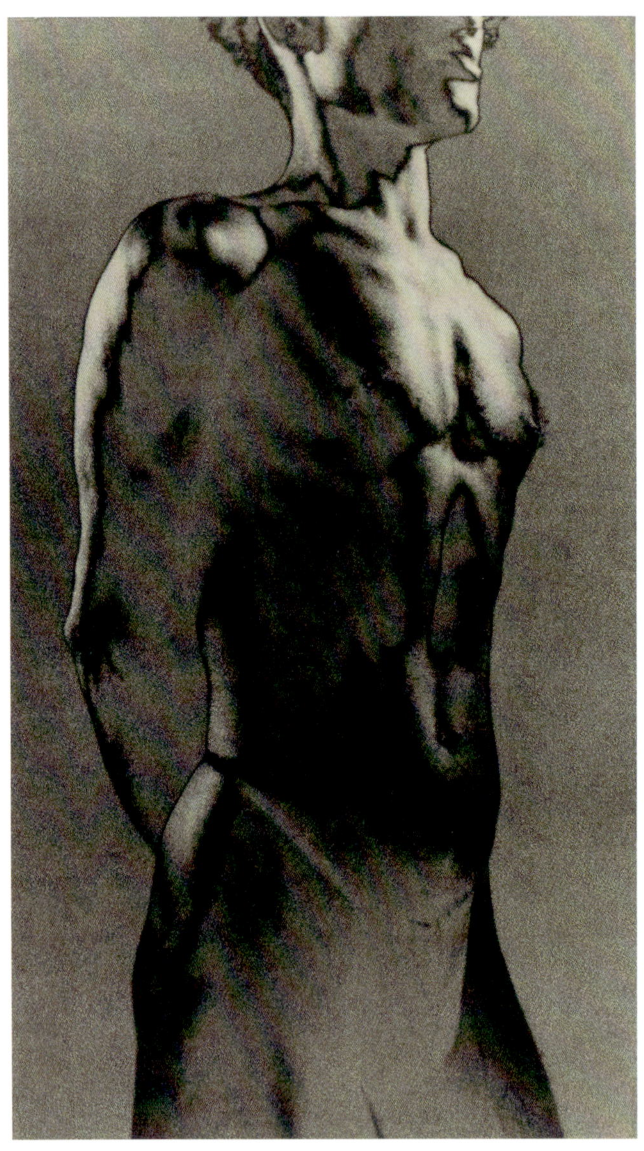

Lionel Wendt

1900–44 Sri Lanka

Untitled

After 1934
Photograph, gelatin silver
print on paper
34.9 x 20.3
Tate. Purchased with funds
provided by the South Asia
Acquisitions Committee 2013

If there's one image that has come to epitomise the desirable male body, it's a muscled, naked torso, photographed in close-up. It's a template put to constant use, from high-end advertising and works by celebrated gay photographers to a million selfies circulating on online dating platforms. Faces are optional, but the six-pack is mandatory. The ubiquitous motif is nowadays under scrutiny, charged with propagating body image anxieties among young men. Yet at one time, it was a novelty. This photograph, taken in Sri Lanka in the 1930s, shows the formula taking shape.

The tight framing of Lionel Wendt's *Untitled* crops the model's body at critical latitudes: the cheekbones and just below the crotch – the zone between is already being identified as what really counts. The discovery that fantasy could be unleashed more effectively by a fragment of the body is one of the key developments in the modern erotic image – and it owes much to some ancient sources. By the early twentieth century, photographs of Greek and Roman sculptures were easily available. Monochrome reproduction, if anything, magnified the seductive appeal of the classical male nude and, in particular, those all-important athletic torsos. For many queer viewers, these marble and bronze bodies with their swelling pectorals and rippling abs became the measure of physical perfection, no matter if heads or limbs were missing.

In *Untitled*, Wendt almost transforms his live model into a classical sculptural fragment. The young man's build is Herculean in comparison to the standards of earlier homoerotic photography (if slender in the eyes of our steroid-enhanced century). His bronze-like sheen is intensified by an effect known as solarisation, where the tones of the camera negative are partially reversed by introducing light during the development process.

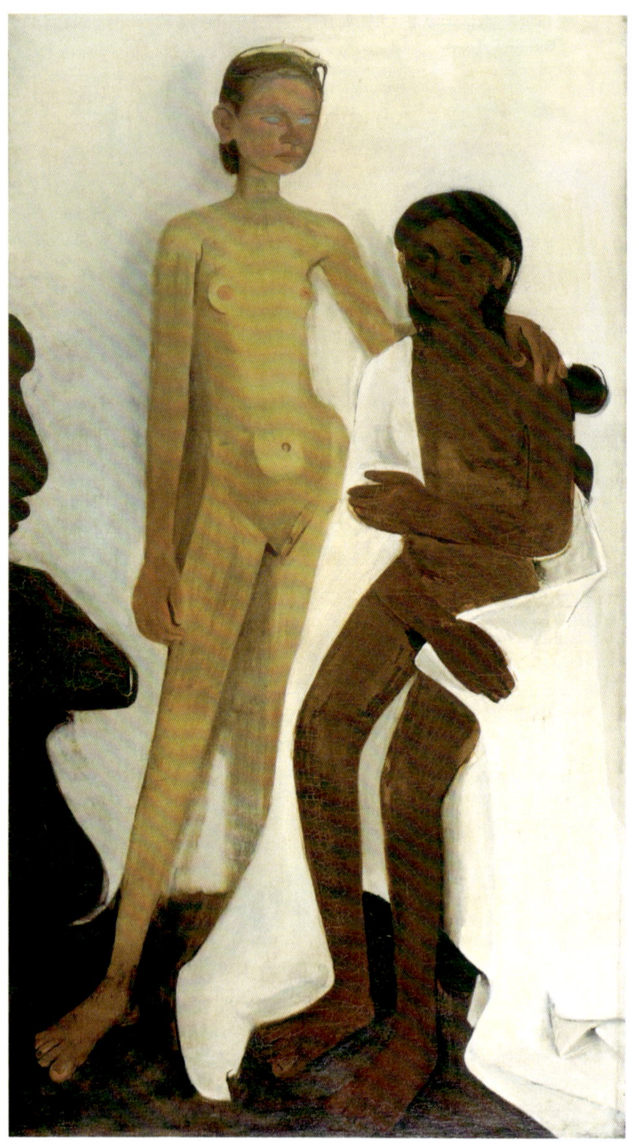

Amrita Sher-Gil
b.1913 Hungary
d.1941 India
Two Girls

c.1939
Oil paint on canvas
158 x 90
Private collection

Two paintings. Four lovers. Six women. Amrita Sher-Gil and Frida Kahlo have become so entangled in the perception of their work that both now haunt their own paintings – nowhere more so than in Sher-Gil's *Two Girls* and Kahlo's *Two Nudes in the Forest* (pp.60–1). Painted in the same year on different continents, these works are coincidental cousins. Little is known about their origins and none of the nude figures can be identified – they certainly don't resemble either artist. So why does prevailing wisdom hold that each work is a symbolic self-portrait?

One persistent gender bias in art criticism is a tendency to link work made by women to details of the artists' life stories. Art historians are fond of interpreting female figures in artworks as stand-ins for their female creators. And if a painting happens to show two women, why not argue that this expresses the artist's divided ego? As both Sher-Gil and Kahlo had mixed heritage, it is commonly claimed that each pair of nudes embodies the dual ethnicity of the artist concerned. The lodestone for such analyses is Kahlo's celebrated double self-portrait, *The Two Fridas* (also 1939).[17] The painted Fridas are twins in culturally distinct costumes: one dressed in Mexican style, the other in European. In contrast to the women in *Two Nudes in the Forest*, they are evident self-portraits of Kahlo. The comparisons drawn between *The Two Fridas* and Sher-Gil's *Two Girls* have a weaker basis still. As the reputations of both artists have grown, Sher-Gil has become saddled with the tag line, 'India's Frida Kahlo', though the parallels between these women are few. Beyond roughly contemporary lifespans and a shared reputation for being glamorous, sexually outgoing and bisexual, their lives were wildly different. As painters, they have almost nothing in common. Fusing their identities helps to market the less well-known Sher-Gil, but reading the latter's work via analogy with Kahlo's paintings is a triumph of hype over insight.

When viewed as bi-racial self-portraits, the surface eroticism of these paintings is neutralised. The tender physical contact in each scene implies same-sex love, but many commentators prefer to see it as self-care – one aspect of the artist's identity resting a protective hand on her other half. Considerable interpretive ingenuity has been used to tame both artworks' obtrusive queer charge. Rival readings of each painting do permit an erotic bond between the women, but the same faith in biographical explanations tempts scholars to name real-life lovers. *Two Nudes in a Forest* is sometimes said to feature Kahlo's friend and possible lover, film star Dolores del Río (1904–83), to whom the painter gave the finished work. (As neither nude resembles del Río any more than the artist, there's no consensus over which is which.) Meanwhile, Sher-Gil's rumoured relationships with one or more white women feed speculation over the couple in *Two Girls*. The fact that the seated, darker woman bears no resemblance to the artist should make us wary of treating this major work as an autobiographical statement.

The favoured biographical interpretations appear to assume that female artists don't create purely imaginative images of love between women. Yet invented lesbian scenes pepper Western art of the last two centuries. And one category of artist has been able to plough this field without arousing any curiosity about their personal relationship history: men.

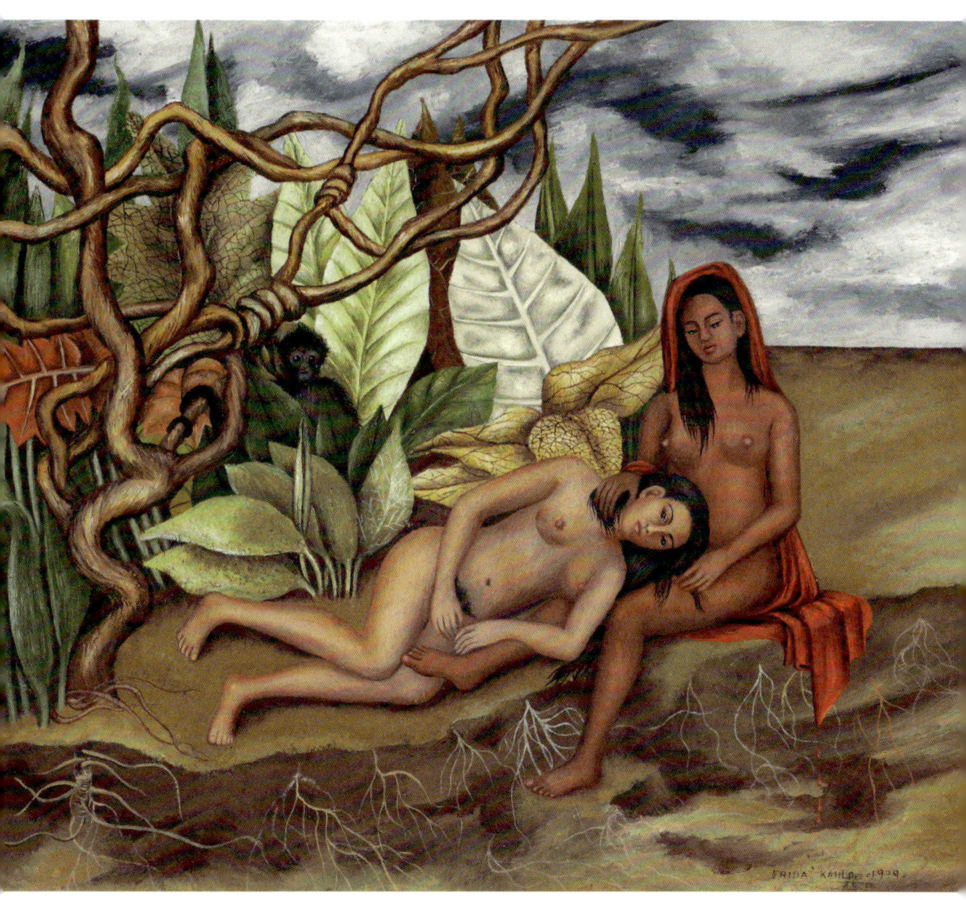

FRIDA KAHLO 1939

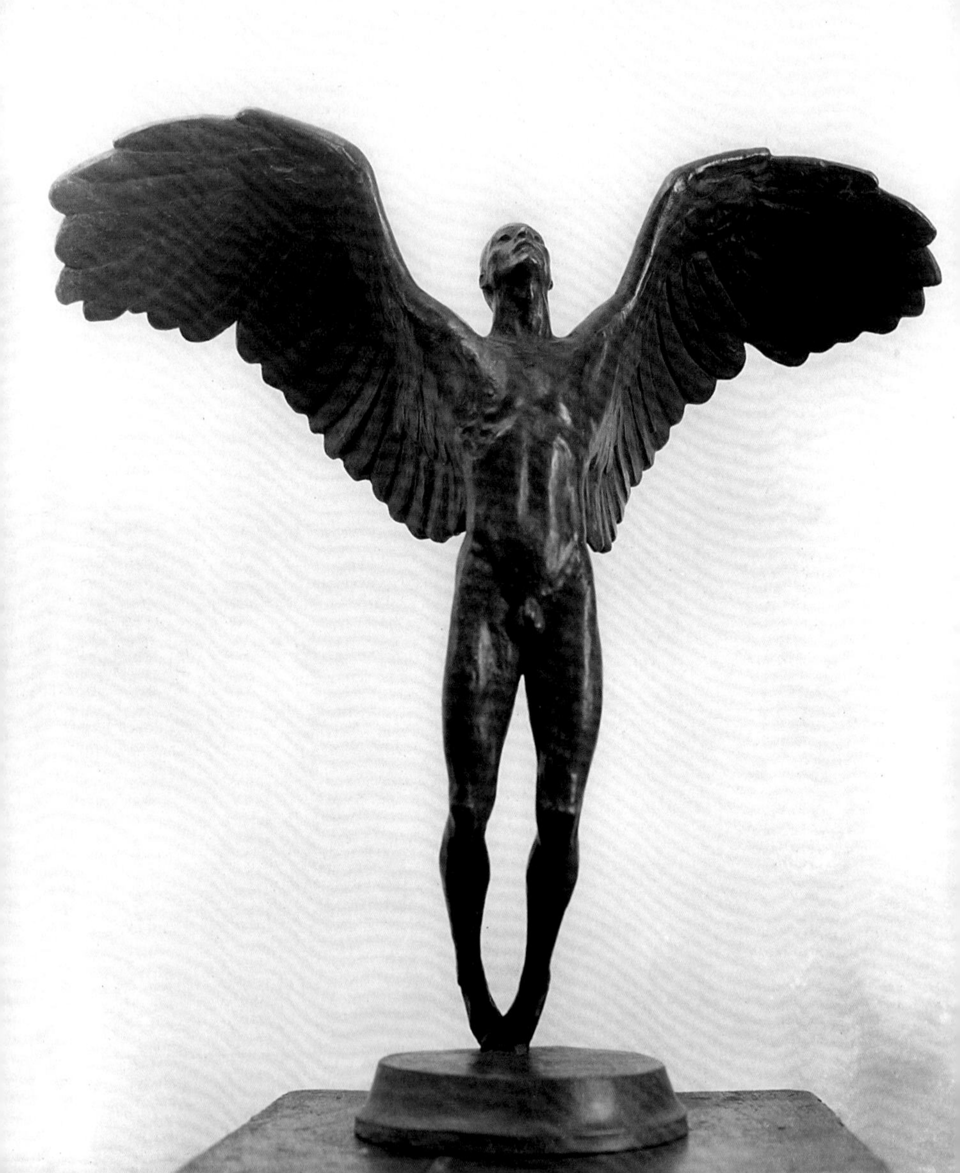

James Richmond Barthé
1909–89 USA
Fallen Aviator

1945
Bronze
47.6 cm (height)
Collection of the Tuskegee
Institute, Tuskegee, Alabama

Fallen Aviator is a memorial to one of the Tuskegee Airmen: the first African-American pilots to be accepted into America's segregated military forces. From 1941, black pilots began to be trained – under the supervision of a white officer class – at a purpose-built airfield attached to the Tuskegee Institute in Alabama. Though the experiment represented a small concession towards equality, the American system of apartheid was still enforced at Tuskegee. Black and white airmen were not even allowed to mingle in the camp cinema.

It is to one of the white officers involved in the programme that we owe Richmond Barthé's *Fallen Aviator*. Years later, the American sculptor revealed that the commission had come from such a source, but neither the name of the patron nor that of his fallen black comrade are known.[18] The motives that lay behind the commission are left for us to guess at; the fact this officer approached a gay, black artist to memorialise his friend might nevertheless be taken as a major clue. Were these two pilots doing some radical desegregation in their off-duty time?

Even if he was more discreet about his sexuality than some of the other gay artists or writers associated with the Harlem Renaissance, Barthé had few qualms about using the male nude to great sensual effect. Part angel, part Icarus, part eagle spirit (the artist had Native-American heritage), the bird-man of *Fallen Aviator* strains every sinew of his hybrid body in a hunger to reach the clouds.

John Craxton
1922–2009 UK
Pastoral for P.W.

1948
Oil paint on canvas
204.5 x 262.6
Tate. Purchased 1984

Painted by one gay man in affectionate tribute to another, *Pastoral for P.W.* testifies to the importance of mid twentieth-century queer networks. The 'P. W.' was Peter Watson (1908–56) – wealthy aesthete and founder of London's Institute of Contemporary Arts as well as Craxton's friend and generous patron. Watson had an international circle almost coextensive with the fabled 'Homintern' – about which, peevish heterosexual contemporaries regularly complained.[19] The irony is that, if queer artistic types *were* often thrown together, it was thanks to that same, pervasive homophobia more than any alleged favouritism.

The gay sensibility encoded in *Pastoral for P.W.* runs much deeper than the shaded crease in those white bell-bottoms, neatly marking the curve of a buttock. Craxton taps a vein of homoerotic Arcadian fantasy running so far back in European culture even the artist was likely unaware of its full sway.[20] From the time of Greek lyric poet Theocritus (third century BC), the tradition of pastoral verse was riddled with rustic bosoms sighing with love or lust over fellow shepherds and goatherds. While these poetic conceits bled into modern homosexual culture in the poems of Oscar Wilde (1854–1900) and Walt Whitman (1819–92), they also shaped queer art well into the twentieth century. Pioneers of homoerotic photography, Wilhelm von Gloeden (1856–1931) and Fred Holland Day (1864–1933) often posed their youthful models in countryside settings, with wooden flutes or panpipes for accessories. Romantic notions of love in the hills, away from the harsh moral and legal codes of civilisation, held understandable appeal for gay men while homosexuality remained under strict prohibition. Craxton himself described his 'entirely imaginary' landscapes with shepherds as 'my means of escape and a sort of self-protection'.[21]

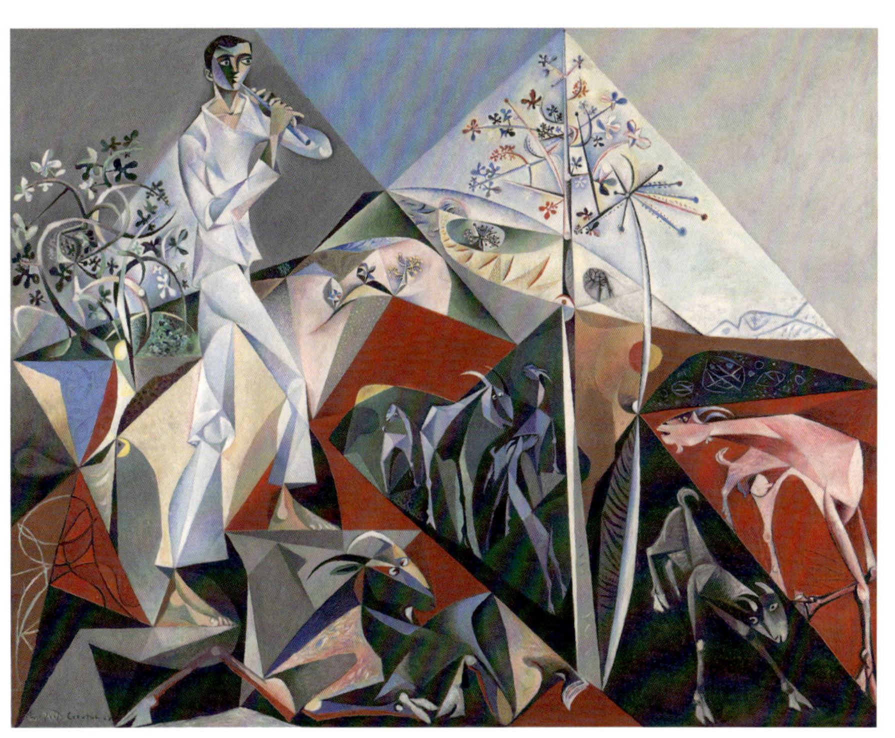

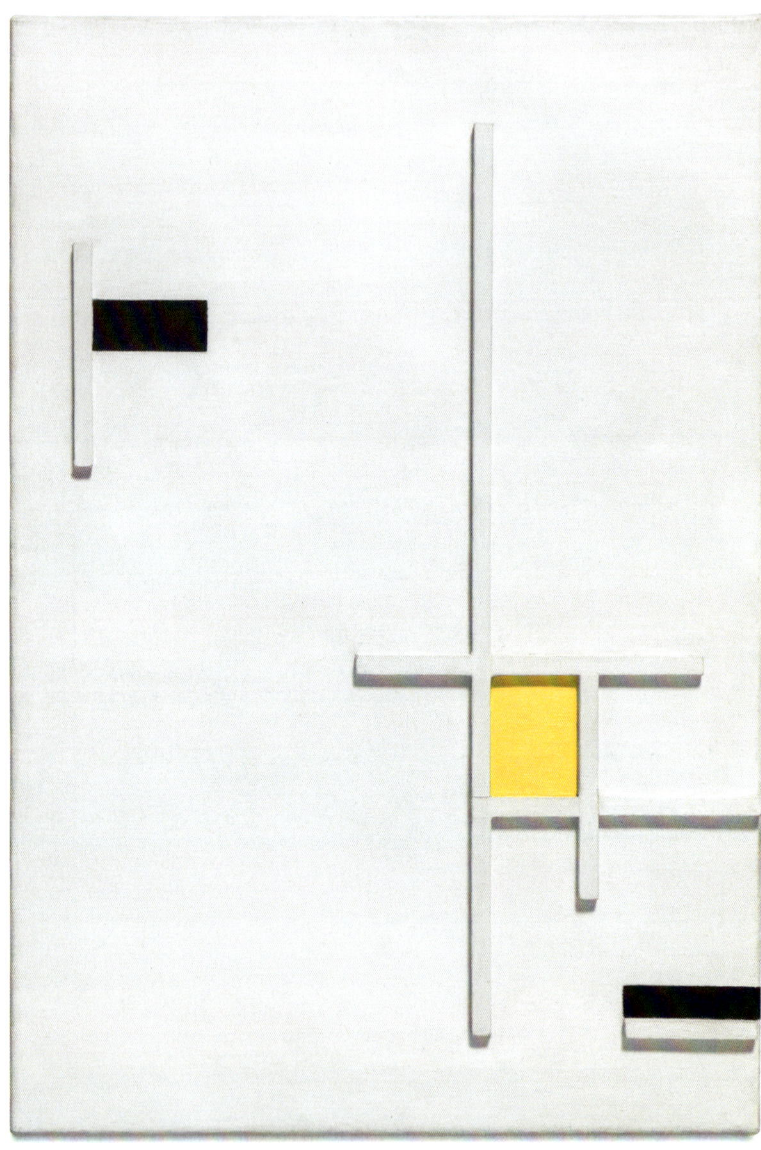

Marlow Moss

1889–1958 UK
*Composition in Yellow,
Black and White*

1949
Oil paint and wood on canvas
50.8 x 35.6 x 0.6
Tate. Presented by
Miss Erica Brausen 1969

A line has no gender. Neither does shape or colour. Gender does not reside in a hairstyle, a name or even a body. And yet, the human social world continues to persuade us that people, clothes, colours and even works of art are either 'feminine', 'masculine' or a blend of the two. Each choice we make about how we look or act, what we wear or create, is assigned a gendered reading under this polarising doctrine.

Marlow Moss trod a defiant course through this territory. The adopted first name, which the artist preferred to use without a title, seems to dodge gender associations. With fastidiously cropped hair, Moss dressed in a style that appeared to some as manly, others as butch or perhaps androgynous. People often took Moss to be male, but records suggest that intimates, including life-partner Netty Nijhoff (1897–1971), referred to the artist with female pronouns. Any attempt to position Moss's gender focuses attention on how slippery such clues are – and all the more so in the past.

And then there is the work. After moving to Paris in 1927, Moss became wedded to a severe, geometric strand of non-objective painting, to an extent unmatched by any British contemporary. Straight lines, primary colours and black rectangles are not actually 'masculine', any more than Marie Laurencin's sploshy pastels are 'feminine' (pp.36–7), but that hasn't stopped critics, past and present, from positioning either style on a spectrum of gender. Is it legitimate to wonder whether Moss consciously 'wore' hard-edged abstraction – such as their favoured tailored jackets, cravats and jodhpurs – as a strategy to disrupt the gender first assigned to them?

Ruth Bernhard
b.1905 Germany
d.2006 USA
Two Leaves

1952, printed c.1952
Photograph, gelatin silver
print on paper
35 × 26
Princeton University Art Museum

In a rebuff to the cliché about the supposed resemblance between flowers and female genitals, this photographic study suggests people have focused on the wrong part of plants all along. With their glistening, veined surfaces, deep central crease and rippling edges, Ruth Bernhard's *Two Leaves* – perhaps from some type of laurel – are giving off a strong scent of sex. When Bernhard moved to New York from her native Berlin in 1927, she found cultured lesbian friends and female lovers. The latter included designer Eveline Phimister, who the bisexual photographer stayed with for around ten years. *Two Leaves* dates from the time of that relationship.

From the 1930s, the time of her first mature works, Bernhard was closely allied to the modernist aesthetic of West Coast photographers such as Edward Weston (1886–1958), Imogen Cunningham (1883–1976) and Ansel Adams (1902–84). This new, 'pure' photography made no attempt to emulate painting and emphasised meticulous composition and sharp detail. Bernhard became best known for her stylishly arranged images of the female nude. Bernhard's early nudes are not obviously erotic, unlike her equally precise nature studies (think close-ups of clam shells). It was only with her 1963 photograph *Two Forms* that she felt able to show the naked torsos of two women in an intimate embrace; the models were a couple known to the photographer. *Two Leaves* is almost a discreet rehearsal for that now-famous image of the following decade.

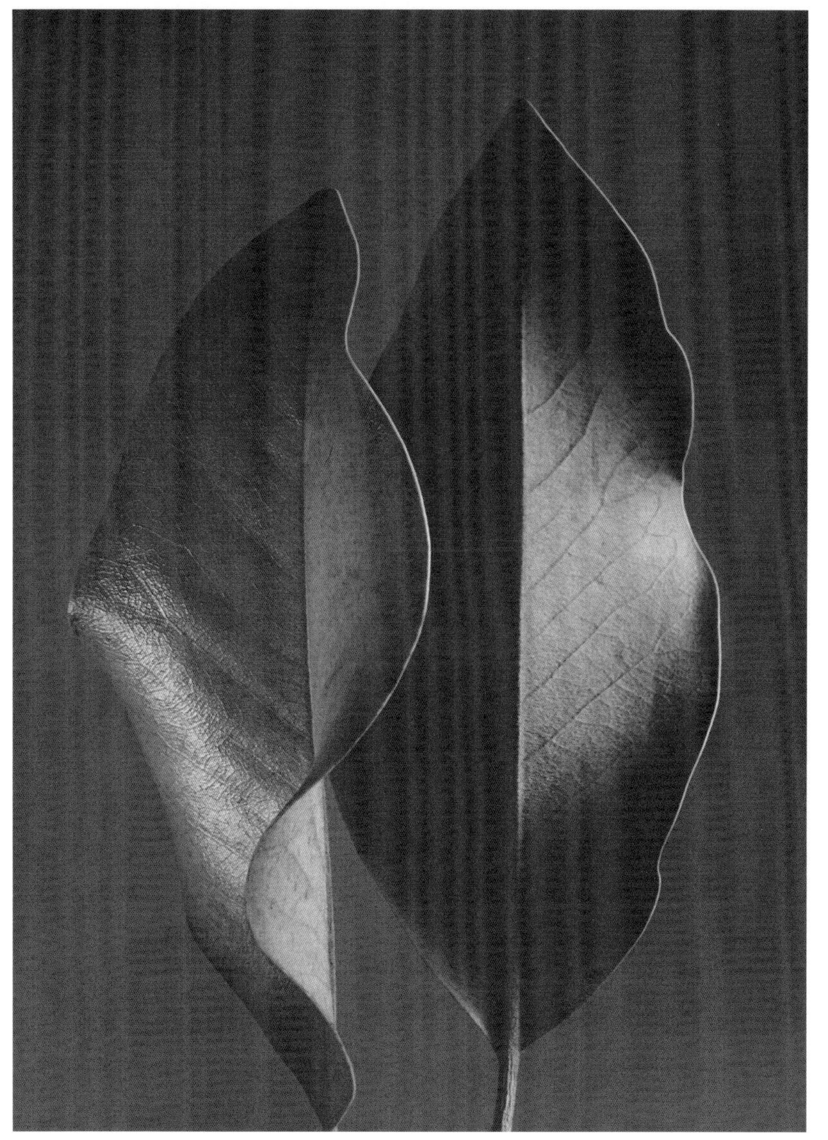

Andy Warhol
1928–87 USA
Male Nude

c.1957
Gold leaf and ink on
coloured paper
43.2 x 35.6
The Andy Warhol Museum,
Pittsburgh

Before Andy Warhol, the famous pop artist who aspired 'to be a machine', there was Andy Warhol, the commercial illustrator aspiring towards artistic recognition.[22] Moving to New York in 1949, Warhol quickly amassed clients, eager for his playful designs with their trademark blotted-ink outlines. He employed the same technique in side projects of the 1950s, destined for gallery shows, artist's books or personal enjoyment. Daring public censure, Warhol worked on homoerotic drawings for all three ends: a queer twist in the decade's repressive narrative. Dozens of sheets are filled with beautiful young men – naked bodies often lovingly embellished with stars, flowers or seashells. Warhol was keen to show off his boy drawings, putting on one exhibition of *Studies for a Boy Book* in 1956.[23] (Other overtures to galleries met with embarrassed refusal.)

In Warhol's already efficient production line, his seemingly casual pen sketches were raw material. *Male Nude*, like many of the more polished artworks, was traced from a simple ballpoint drawing.[24] Warhol zooms in on this gilded crotch as though to reveal all (in the manner of Gustave Courbet's infamous 1866 painting, *The Origin of the World*).[25] A unisex tuft of pubic hair is all we find – the central hand's masculine proportions the only hint as to what form of genitals its fingers conceal. Are we observing male modesty or female masturbation? Assurances regarding sexed bodies are challenged by the image's teasing omissions.

Anatomical ambiguity was not typical of Warhol, who enjoyed drawing penises at every opportunity (even decorating them with ribbons and love hearts). Several associates of the 1950s recalled a common approach to any man who interested him: 'let me draw your cock. I'm doing a cock book.'[26]

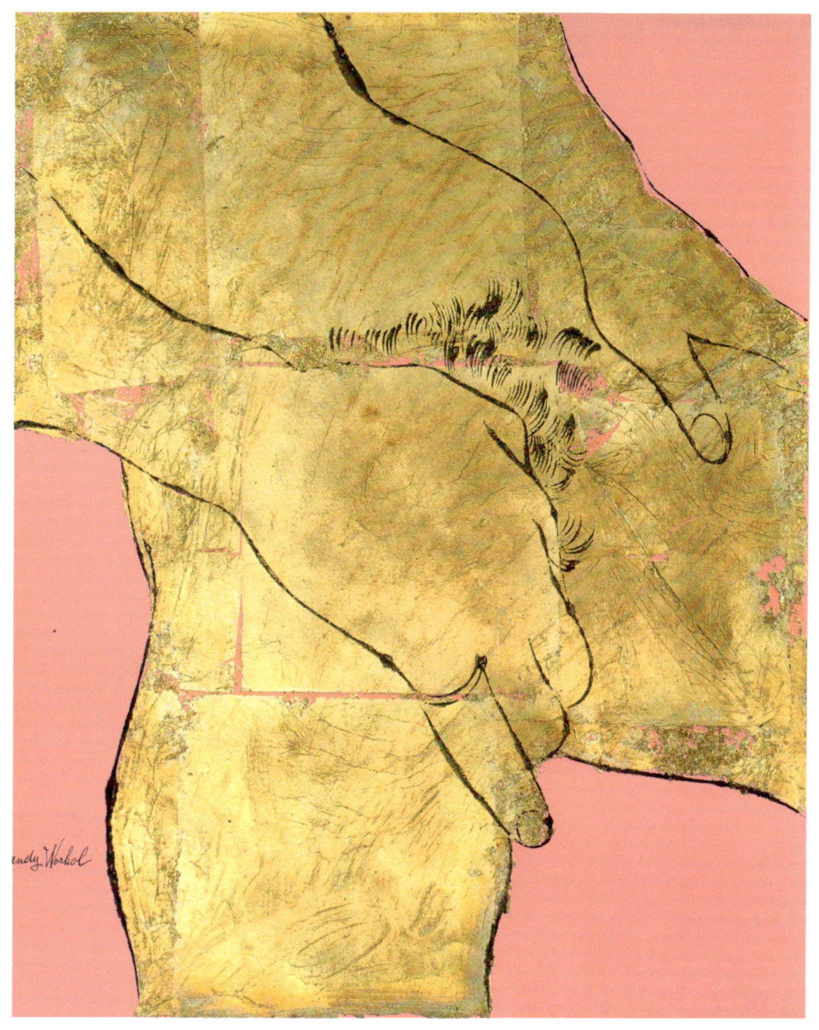

Andy Warhol

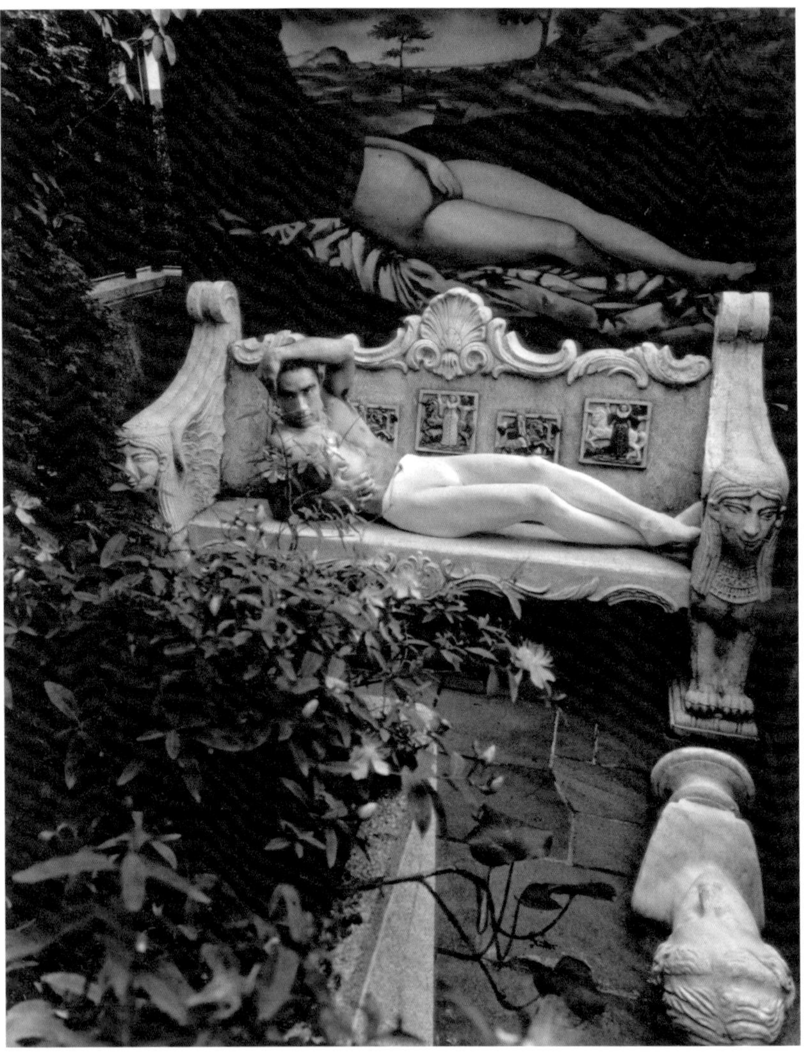

Eikoh Hosoe
b.1933 Japan
Ordeal by Roses #41
Bara-kei

1961
Photograph, gelatin
silver print on paper
27.9 x 35.5
Yodo Gallery, Osaka

The figure glowering from that extraordinary seat is author Yukio Mishima (1925–70). In 1961 – inspired following a portrait sitting with the writer – photographer Eikoh Hosoe initiated a six-month collaboration on a series of dreamlike images: the basis for his exquisite photo book, *Ordeal by Roses* (1963).[27]

Mishima's complex obsession with the male body combined reverence for bygone samurai values, a fascination with male nudes in Western art, and a very modern interest in bodybuilding. The author took up physical training aged thirty and, attaining the body shape he'd idealised, 'wanted to display it to everyone … to let it move in front of every eye'.[28] *Ordeal by Roses* was a theatrical first outing. Mishima continued to glorify his body with help from other photographers, including Kishin Shinoyama (b.1940), for whom he famously posed as St Sebastian, and pioneer homoerotic photographer Tamotsu Yato (1928–73). Such images fed the emerging macho aesthetic in Japanese homoerotica. The gay illustrator Goh Mishima (1921–89) – known for his tattoed musclemen in bondage – even adopted the writer's pseudonym, after befriending Mishima at a gym.

In *Ordeal by Roses*, Mishima generally wears a loincoth. Here, he reclines in ballet tights and, from the waist down, assumes the pose of the painted Renaissance Venus in the background.[29] Just as that surreal replica truncates the goddess at the waist, so Mishima's feminine masquerade ends at the hips; arms and torso are tensed to show off his masculine physique. For all its virtuosity, this baroque photograph was omitted from the 1963 book. Perhaps its subject felt uncomfortable with this, one of the queerer images in Hosoe's portfolio.

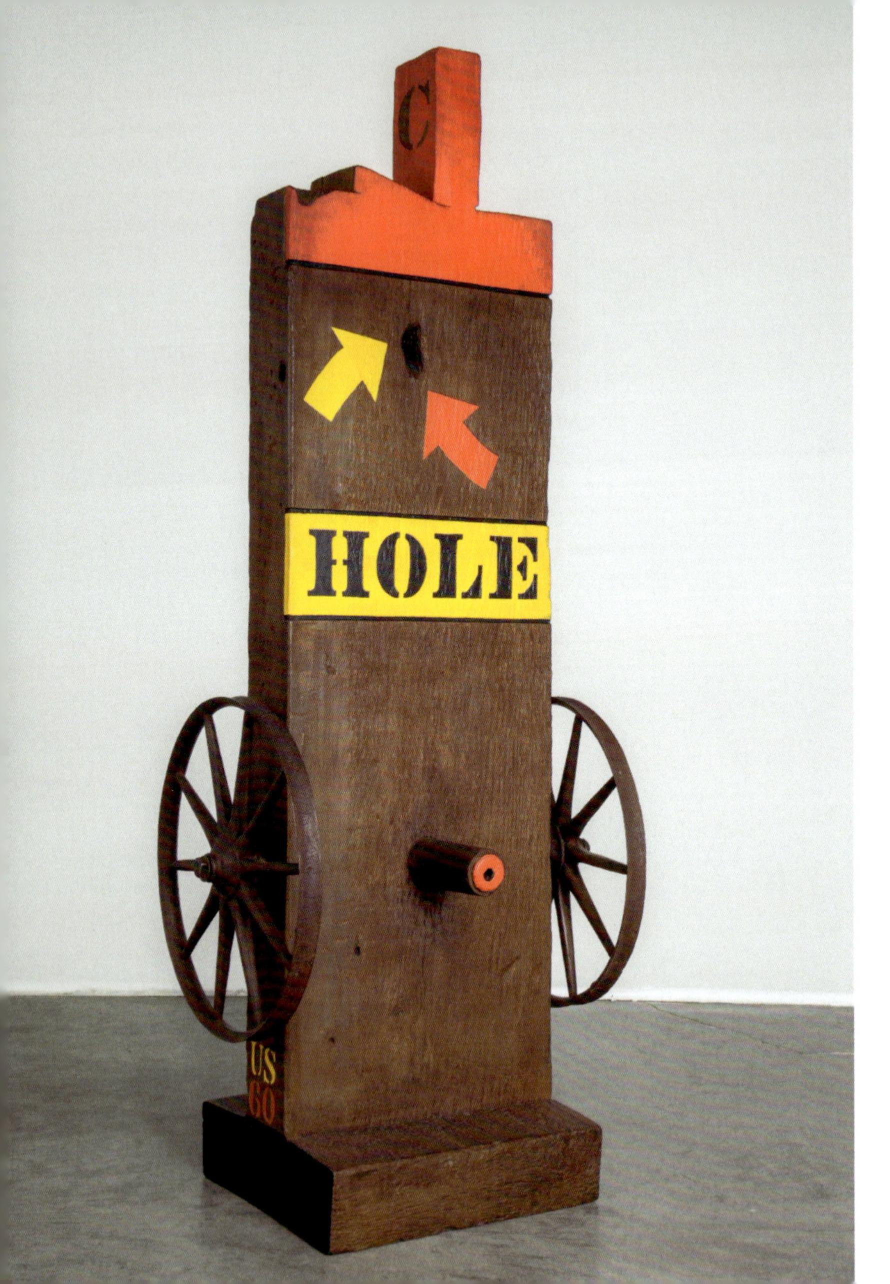
C
HOLE
US
60

Robert Indiana

1928–2018 USA

Hole

1960/1991
Painted bronze cast of original
115.6 x 49.5 x 34.2
Private collection

Hole dates from the moment Robert Indiana was arriving at his mature artistic identity: 'an American painter of signs'.[30] In 1956, the artist moved into a run-down industrial loft near the southern tip of Manhattan, on Coenties Slip. With studio space cheap, the slip attracted a community of artists: mostly young, often gay, all at odds with abstract expressionism (still dominating American art).[31] The ingredients of Indiana's style – geometric shapes, intense colour, resonant inscriptions with ambiguous meanings – first came together in this creative, queer-friendly environment.

Free materials abounded. Indiana began harvesting beams from demolition sites to fashion into standing sculptures, which he nicknamed 'herms'. The ancient Greek herm, a type of wayside marker, was a vertical stone block topped with the head of a male god. The only other body parts, carved on the otherwise flat front, were genitals, often with a large, erect penis. The round pegs that jut from the lower regions of Indiana's herms are an irreverant take on their phallic Greek prototypes; these sculptures literally have a woody. There are further masculine protuberances. The only form of 'head' on Indiana's herms are long tenons: the 'male' sides of the joints that once locked these beams together.[32]

The pithy, stencilled titles on many of these works invoke bodily or sexual connotations: *Orb* (1960), *Mate* (1960–2), *Eat* (1962) and *Hole*. Juxtaposed with the herms' eager wooden members, these are signs towards queer destinations for whoever cared to read them. Through his playful, almost abstract forms, Indiana celebrated the sexual appeal of male bodies under the noses of New York gallery goers.

Marisol
b.1930 France
d.2016 USA
Women and Dog

1963–4
Wood, plaster, synthetic polymer
and taxidermied dog head
186.8 x 194.6 x 67.9
Whitney Museum of American Art,
New York

A drawback of photographic reproduction is that one standardised viewpoint often comes to define our perception of sculptures, at the expense of all other potential angles. Take Marisol's *Women and Dog*. A widespread interpretation sees this work as a satire on conventional gender roles. The women's conservative fashions are taken as evidence that they are 'housewives' and the butt of Marisol's feminist critique. Finally, their boxed torsos and mask-like faces symbolise how women's potential is confined by society's expectations. It all sounds fairly conclusive … until you walk round to the back. From here, you discover that the central woman has a hand on each of her companions, her left one brushing the top of her friend's backside. Her own pink buttocks are mysteriously exposed by a kidney-shaped opening in the seat of her green skirt. Shifting our viewpoint reveals clues to an erotic connection between these women, not obvious from the frontal view shown in published photographs.

Like the rear view of *Women and Dog*, the queer dimensions of Marisol's art have been generally neglected. Established, heterosexual feminist interpretations of this artist tend to characterise her as a stern critic: the Betty Friedan (1921–2006) of pop art. This perhaps does her some disservice. A queer-centred take on Marisol might uncover a liberating, even joyous, sense of possibility in works such as *Untitled, Box [Kiss]* (1960, Abrams Family Collection), where two faces press lipsticked mouths together, or *The Wedding* (1962–3, private collection), where both bride and 'groom' have women's faces, or in Marisol's erotic lithographs from the late 1970s, where feminine hands roam over female erogenous zones.

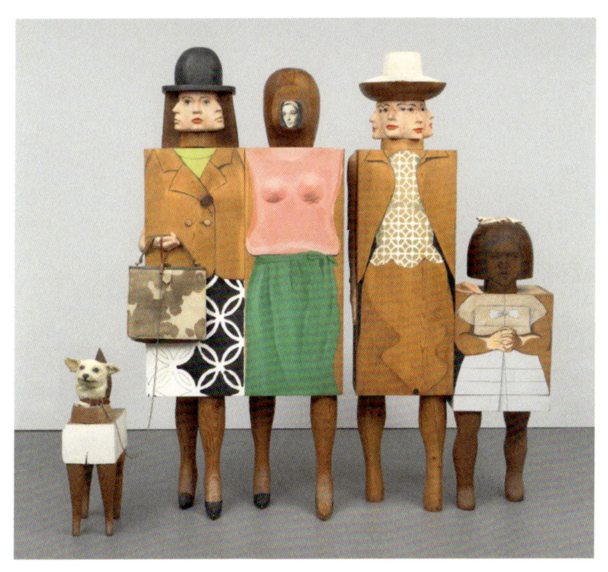

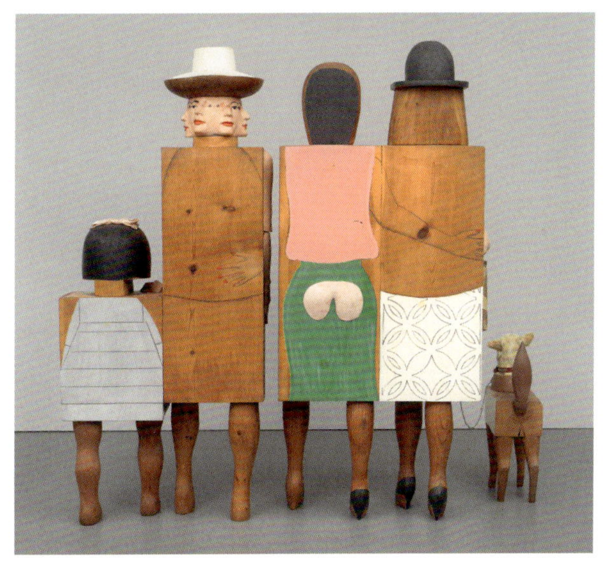

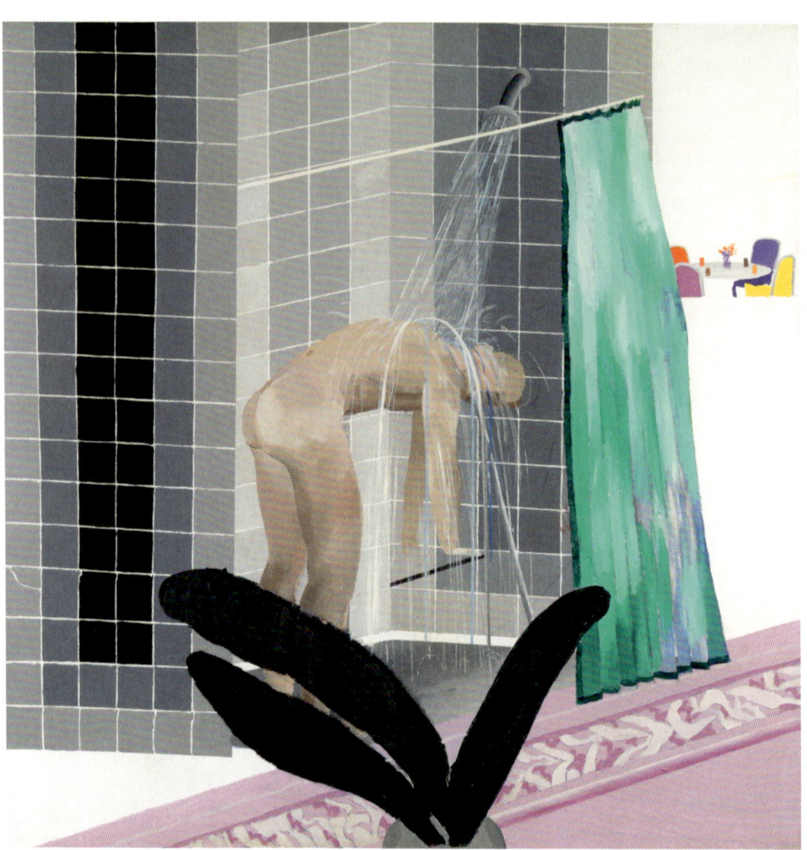

David Hockney

b.1937 UK
*Man in Shower in
Beverly Hills*

1964
Acrylic paint on canvas
167.3 x 167
Tate. Purchased 1980

Bob Mizer (1922–92) may not be a household name, even in queer households, but his influence on Western gay visual culture was profound. Via his Los Angeles studio, Athletic Model Guild (founded 1945) and his magazine, *Physique Pictorial* (1951–91), Mizer championed homoerotic photography in post-war America. His images of muscle-bound, oiled young men in tiny posing pouches delighted international subscribers and gave macho shape to a new, aspirational gay ideal. Mizer's magazine provided an important platform for gay artists – notably Tom of Finland (1920–91) – and inspiration to others, including Robert Mapplethorpe (1946–89) and Andy Warhol (1928–87).

One subscriber in the early 1960s was David Hockney, then a student at London's Royal College of Art. Hockney even painted a bodybuilder from a *Physique Pictorial* photograph as an examination piece (*Life Painting for a Diploma* 1962), having unsuccessfully complained that the college hired unattractive life models. Mizer's photography nurtured Hockney's dream of California as 'a sunny land of … beautiful semi-naked people'.[33] After relocating to Los Angeles in 1964, the artist adopted acrylic paints and created the bright canvases of men in pools, showers and bedrooms that remain among his most recognisable works. Hockney began taking his own photographs of men as working material, but his Californian shower paintings of 1963–4 (the first painted while still in London) borrow their nude figures from the pages of *Physique Pictorial* or, as in this instance, from other Athletic Model Guild photographs.

The large houseplant in *Man in Shower in Beverly Hills* helped the artist out of a 'great difficulty in painting the figure's feet'. It also positions the viewer as a voyeur.[34]

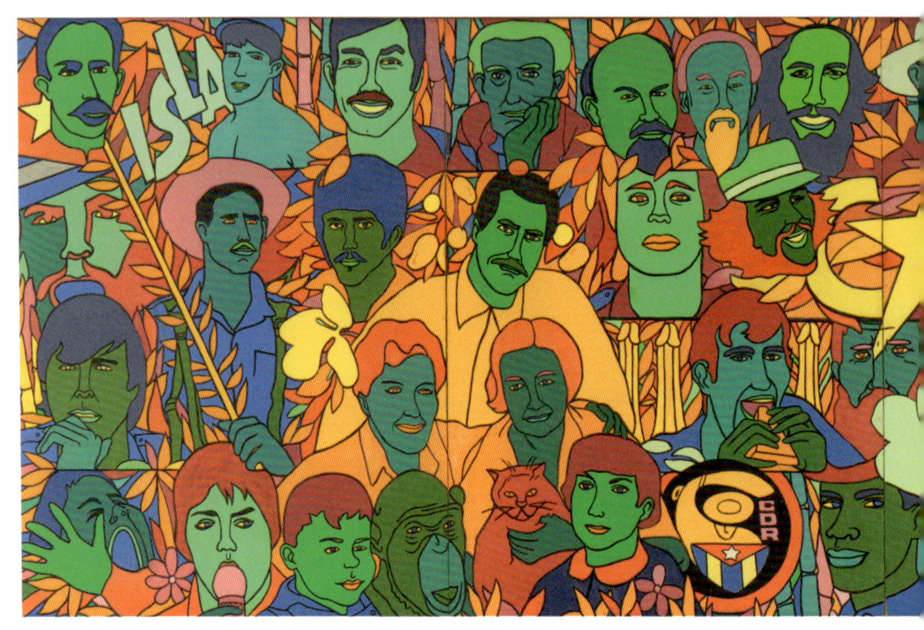

Raúl Martínez

1927–95 Cuba

Island 70

Isla 70

1970
Oil paint on canvas (three panels)
200 x 451
El Museo Nacional de Bellas Artes,
Havana

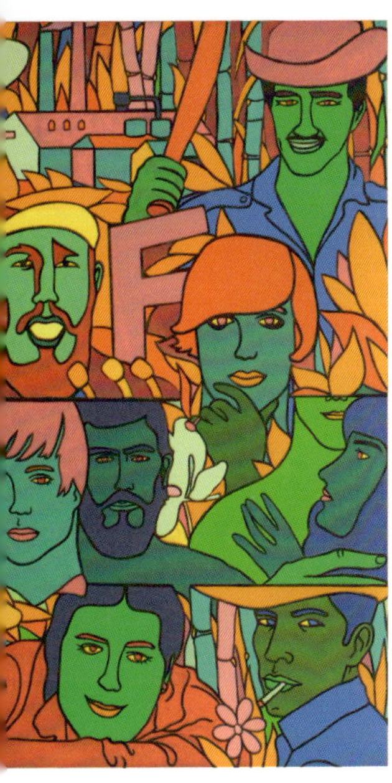

Revolution, mangoes, a touch of sex and a cat: what more could you ask for in an artwork? *Island 70* is an upbeat celebration of Cuba and its people at the end of the first revolutionary decade. The wild colours and heavy outlines resemble contemporary Cuban posters. Raúl Martínez was in fact one of the island's leading graphic designers, yet his paintings only shifted away from abstraction in the late 1960s, mindful of the political mood.

Communist icons Lenin and Ho Chi Minh show up for this party, alongside local revolutionary heroes.[35] Guerrillas rub shoulders with farmers, cowboys and the artist himself, who grins at us from the top row (second from left). 1970 saw a mass mobilisation to raise national sugar output. Sugar cane, appropriately, forms the background to *Island 70*. A mill is glimpsed top-right and at least one patriotic worker has showed up with a machete. But Martínez seems more focused on the dreamy young men with floppy hair, pretty eyes and fluorescent pouts, who don't look like they heard the call for harvest volunteers. One sucks on a strawberry ice cream: a sexual reference almost comically transparent. And the orange-haired cat-owners seem to be a lesbian couple. If this is a grand piece of socialist mural art, it's not what you might expect in a country where homophobia was enshrined in party policy. (The artist, who made no secret of being gay, knew this all too well, having already been purged from his teaching posts.) It's as though Martínez says to us: 'Yes, sugar is important, but in *my* utopia, same-sex love must also be valued.'

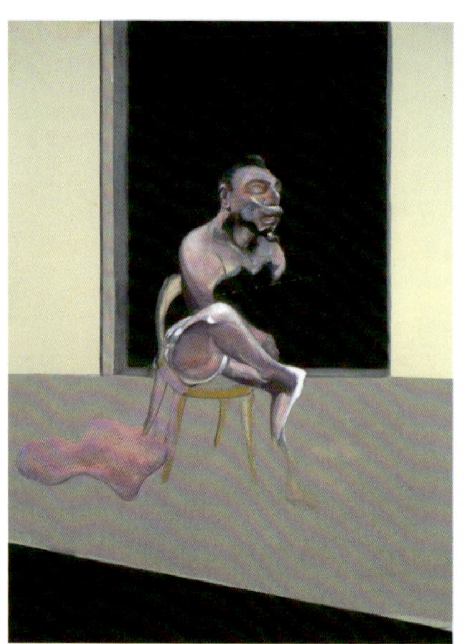 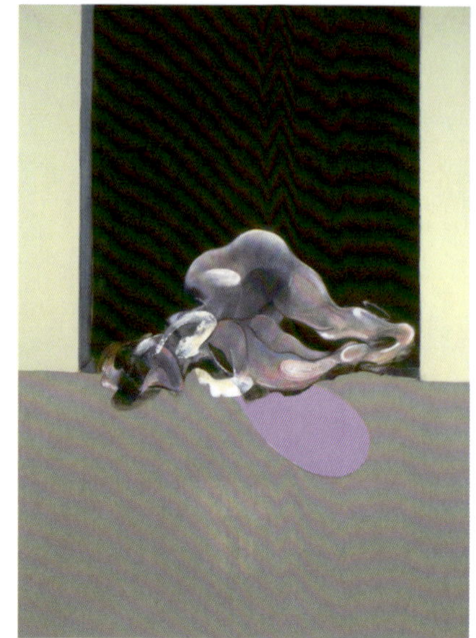

Francis Bacon

b.1909 Ireland

d.1992 Spain

Triptych – August 1972

1972
Oil paint and sand on
three canvases
198.1 x 147.3 (each panel)
Tate. Purchased 1980

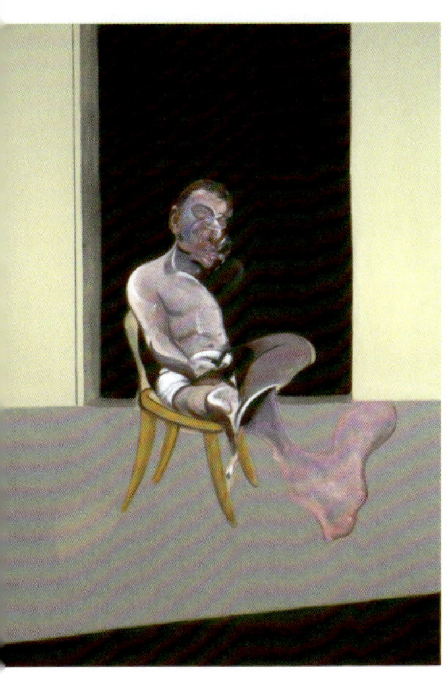

In October 1971, eight years into his relationship with Francis Bacon, George Dyer committed suicide in their shared Paris hotel room. It was two days before the opening of Bacon's most prestigious exhibition to date. Understandably haunted, the artist revisited this tragic episode in subsequent paintings. As he stated to one interviewer during these years, 'all the people I've been really fond of have died. And you don't stop thinking about them; time doesn't heal.'[36]

One of Bacon's habitual painting formats was the triptych (a set of three adjacent panels). *Triptych – August 1972* is the second of three grim memorials to Dyer's unhappy end: the so-called 'black triptychs'. The two side panels draw upon photographs taken years earlier, showing Dyer posing in white underpants in his lover's studio. The quivering mass in the central painting, if characteristically ambiguous, probably recalls their sexual encounters.

In this central image, Bacon returns to a favourite source: a photographic motion sequence of naked male wrestlers, published by Eadweard Muybridge in his landmark *Animal Locomotion* (1887). The painter exploited the homoerotic suggestiveness of these photographs repeatedly, from 1953's confrontational *Two Figures* – where the wrestlers materialise on a bed – to his final *Triptych* of 1991. The wrestling sequence enabled Bacon to paint scenes of queer sexual passion that also supported respectable critical interpretations. Viewing these works, many only perceived a pessimistic commentary on human existence as animalistic struggle. 'The thing is', as Bacon told an art-critic friend, 'unless you look at those Muybridge figures with a magnifying glass, it's very difficult to see whether they're wrestling or having sex.'[37]

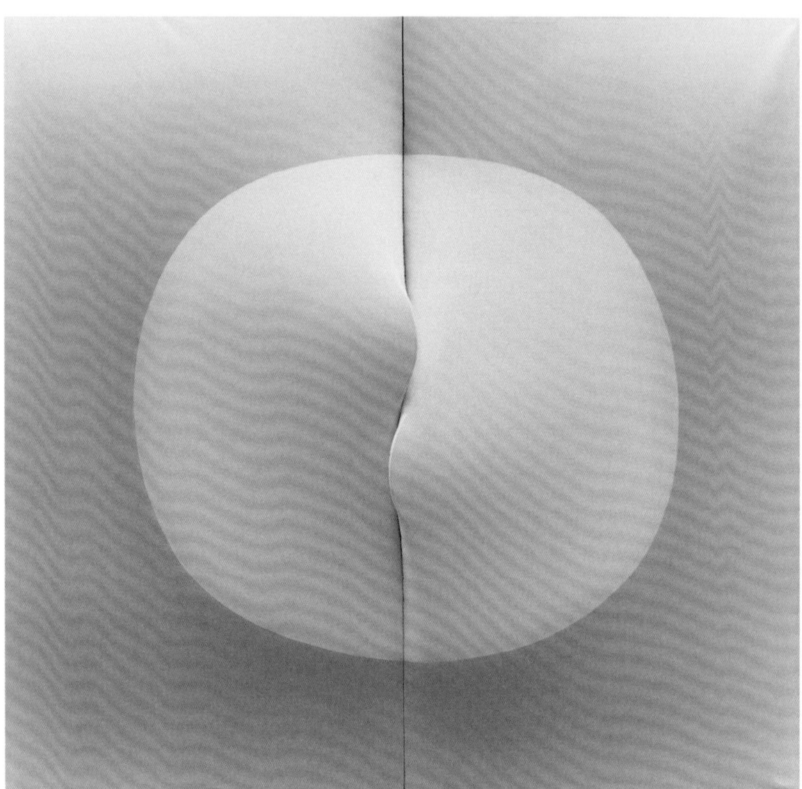

Zilia Sánchez
b.1926 Cuba, lives
Puerto Rico
Moon V
Lunar V

c.1973
Acrylic paint on stretched canvas
189.9 x 201.9 x 25.4
Private collection

Can a language of minimal, abstract forms articulate the sensual interactions between human bodies? The artworks of Zilia Sánchez provoke that question. Each viewer will have their own answer: unanimity, mercifully, not being a feature of humans' erotic sensibility.

Sánchez creates contoured surfaces by stretching her canvas over wooden armatures. With mathematical precision, she divides this skin into zones of colour (often, concentric ellipses). Her paint is flawlessly hard-edged and draws from a trusted pool of cooler shades: white, grey, the palest of pinks, desaturated blues. A palette of four tones is the usual maximum per work and many, including *Moon V*, are limited to two. It's a restricted vocabulary – some might say clinical – but, within these terms, Sánchez includes enough reminders of the human body to justify her own description of these artworks as 'erotic topologies'.

Anatomical references are remarkably pared down. Where the canvases peak in circular plateaus, we might think of erect nipples – surrounding rings of colour hinting at areolae – but the association remains at a purely topological level. Sánchez's colour choices and immaculate paint surfaces offer no fleshy reinforcement. If this art is imbued with an erotic charge, its force derives from this lack of visual signals. The viewer is invited not to observe an explicit image, but to partake in erotic *empathy* with these canvas bodies. Nowhere is this more potent than in the works where two or more components press against each other. There's something quite hot about the interlocking lips of the two parts in *Moon V*, and their precise equivalence is characteristic of this artist's queer erotic symmetries.

Barkley L. Hendricks
1945–2017 USA
Family Jules: NNN
(No Naked Niggahs)

1974
Oil paint on linen
168.1 x 183.2
Tate. Lent by the American Fund
for the Tate Gallery, courtesy of
the North American Acquisitions
Committee 2011

In a gallery of artworks, Barkley L. Hendricks once said, 'I'm damn sure I want you to remember mine'.[38] *Family Jules: NNN (No Naked Niggahs)* tends to win out in any room. While teaching at Yale University, Hendricks got to know the young student Jules Taylor (1952–84) and began asking this 'beautiful, skinny dude' to model for paintings.[39] In their first collaboration, Taylor strikes a sinuous pose, hands thrust into figure-hugging dungarees (*Jules* 1971, private collection). For his fourth portrait, Hendricks asked his six-and-a-half foot friend to pose nude.

Hendricks upgrades his draped studio couch to a faintly Middle-Eastern daybed and completes the setting with Moroccan tiles. The allusion is to the fantasised 'harem' scenes so beloved of European artists, from Jean-Auguste-Dominique Ingres (1780–1867) to Henri Matisse (1869–1954). In place of a hookah, Jules holds a hash pipe. And where an orientalist painter would have inserted a pale, soporific female nude (a so-called 'odalisque'), there sits a gay, stoned, black intellectual. (Fittingly, considering this image's North-African theme, Taylor would go on to study the representation of black people in ancient Egyptian art.)

The presence of another is suggested by a discarded shirt. Lying near the naked Jules, it's a detail that could easily prompt queer scenarios in a viewer's imagination. Hendricks, the real off-stage owner of the shirt, was not gay (and was likely clothed for the job), but the relaxed, queer vibe of this picture speaks of his ease around gay men and nudity alike.[40] Along with its pun on male genitals ('family jewels'), the painting's title pokes fun at cultural anxieties around black nakedness. It's easy to imagine it stemming from a joke shared between artist and model.

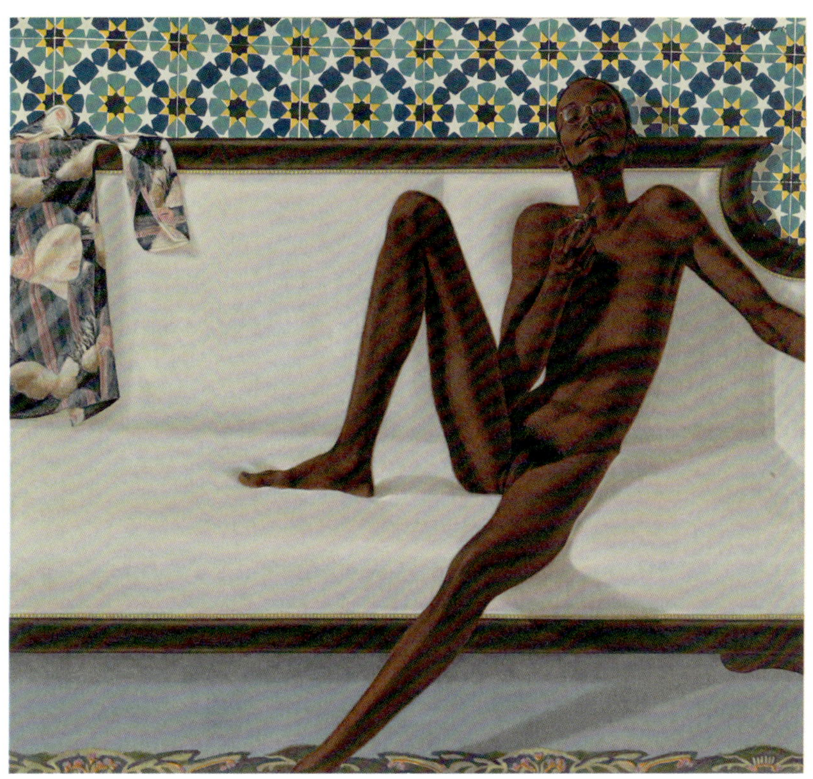

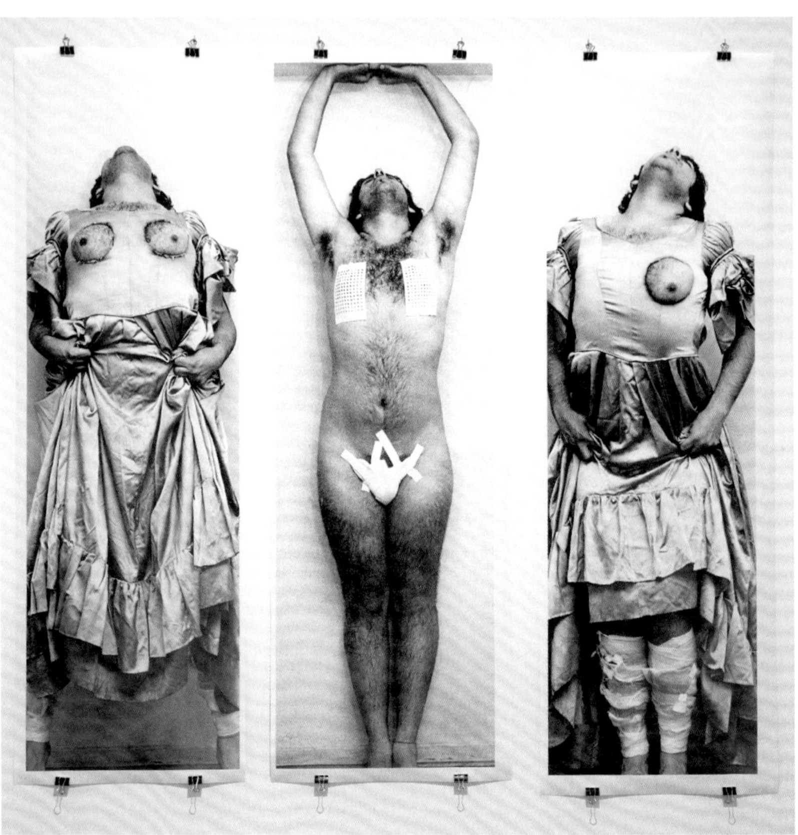

Carlos Leppe
1952–2015 Chile
The Clothes Rack
El perchero

1975, reprinted 2011
Gelatin silver prints on three
sheets of paper (originally
installed with wooden clothes
rack and hangers)
173 x 180 (overall); 173 x 58
(each part)
Museo Nacional Centro de
Arte Reina Sofía, Madrid

In 1975, proclaimed International Women's Year, one Santiago gallery issued a curious invitation to Chile's sculptors. Titled *Senografía*, the competition sought art celebrating the female breast as a symbol of 'important virtues and forces: security, prosperity, and fertility'.[41] The announcement's language signals the impact of Chile's violent shift to the right under the repressive military dictatorship that seized power in 1973. Reactionary regimes often promote an ideal of the placid, maternal, female body as a cornerstone of national order.

Carlos Leppe's entry – reproduced here in its later, simplified form – claimed second prize in this competition. As first assembled, *The Clothes Rack* included a wooden clothes rail and three coat hangers. The large format photographs of the artist were folded over the bars of the hangers, the two ends stapled together, such that the upper part of Leppe's body was viewed (upside down) from one side of the installation and the lower half from the other. The only breasts are Leppe's own, remoulded into surprisingly feminine domes by holes cut through his voluminous satin dress. Shunning most drag conventions, Leppe makes use of his own hairy curves to present a body that challenges binary categorisations of sex. The effect extends to the central photograph, where Leppe stands naked. Here, he conceals his nipples and genitals with what look like medical dressings. Bandaged legs in the flanking images strengthen the impression of a wounded body. This suffering trio, hung from a rail, evokes the fate of thousands of Chileans who disappeared into the junta's torture centres throughout this decade – always in the name, of course, of security and prosperity.

Tee A. Corinne
1943–2006 USA
Untitled

1976, published 1977
Solarised photograph
Dimensions unknown
University of Oregon Libraries,
Special Collections &
University Archives

The images that surround us tend to resonate with the present orchestration of society; hence, profound revolutions demand images in new modes. Rarely has this been so evident as during the feminist revolution. Images produced under patriarchy for centuries rehearsed a narrow, disempowering range of roles for women. In the 1970s, artists aligned with the women's liberation movement in Western countries deployed new visual strategies to break that cycle.

Some artists avoided representing the female body altogether, feeling such images compromised under male domination. Others sought to undo women's shame and ignorance about their bodies by celebrating sexual anatomy, whether in abstracted 'central core imagery' or in realistic detail. Tee Corinne was responsible for one memorable example of the latter: a collection of outline drawings published in 1975 as *The Cunt Coloring Book*. Corinne also pioneered what would become the most contentious strand of feminist art: explicit lesbian erotic photography. Her images proved popular with their target audience, appearing in many lesbian publications in the late 1970s and 1980s. Yet they were also rejected by some titles, declining to print what they saw as pornography.

This image of two women having sex first appeared on a cover of the lesbian journal *Sinister Wisdom*. A poster version followed, in response to reader demand, and became a fixture in lesbian homes and women's bookstores – the queer, American pin-up of its day. Corinne, like Lionel Wendt (pp.56–7), used solarisation (the partial reversal of tones in a photograph) in much of her erotic art, but here it becomes a political tool. Corinne's solarisation is intended to deny pleasure to the objectifying masculine gaze, reserving the explicit lesbian image for lesbian consumption.

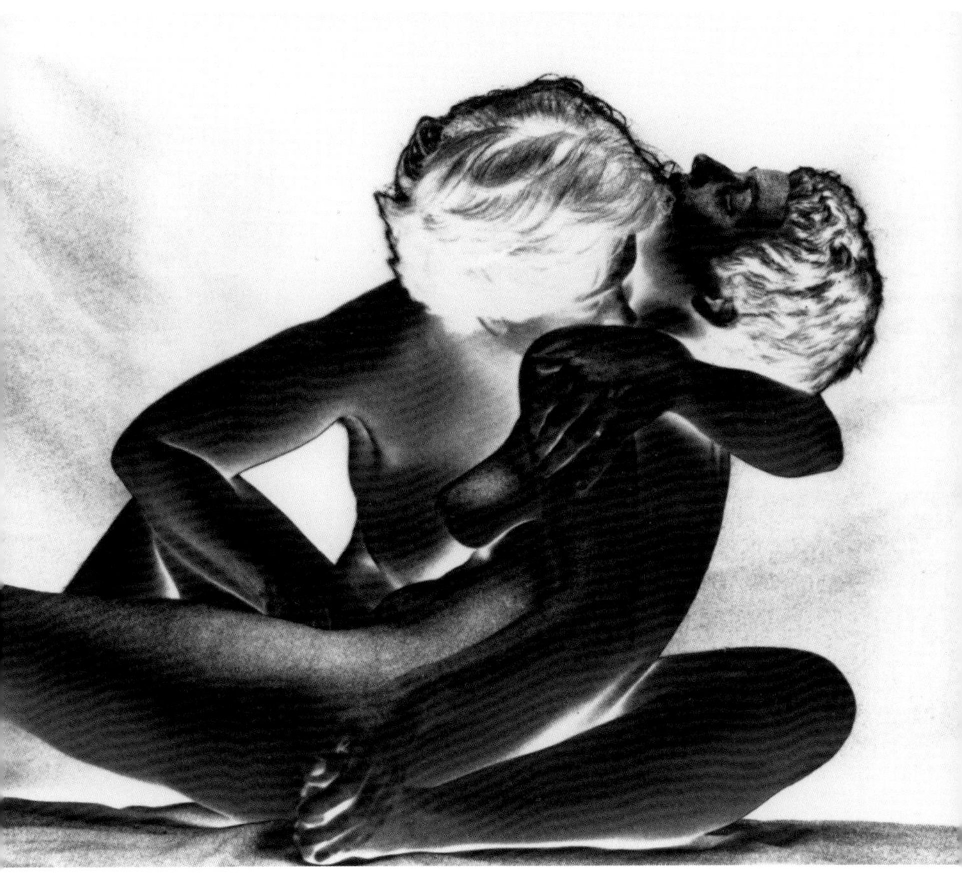

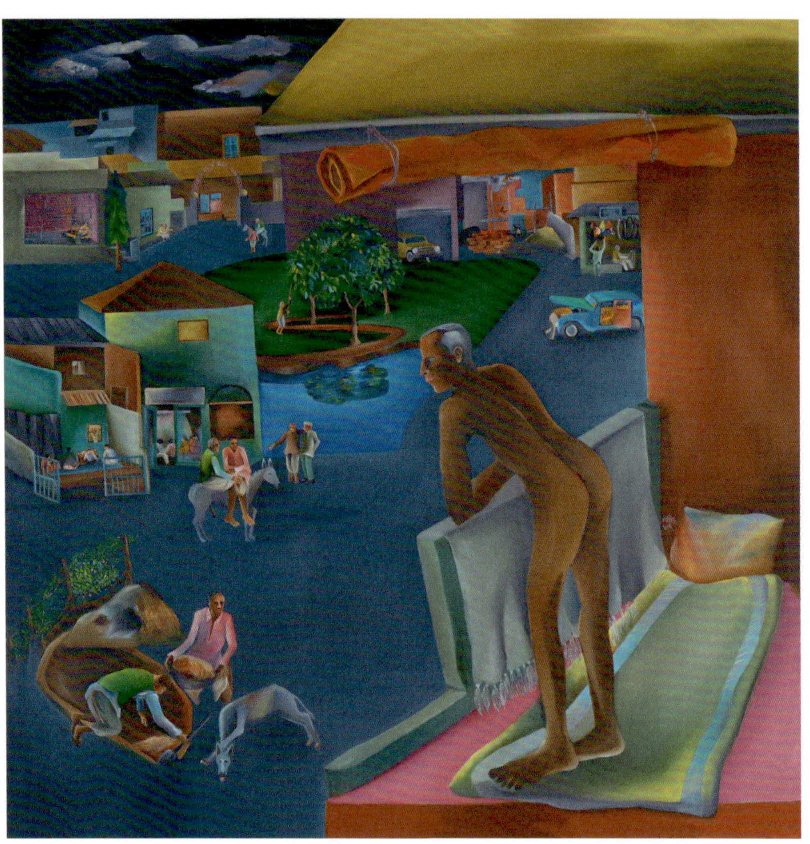

Bhupen Khakhar

1934–2003 India
You Can't Please All

1981
Oil paint on canvas
175.6 x 175.6
Tate. Purchased 1996

Here's a town with an ass problem. The townsfolk, busy with daily life, are unaware of anything awry. It's two men passing through who wrestle with the donkey issue alone. Their sorry tale teaches us a moral: you can't please all.

Bhupen Khakhar's own troubles did not concern a donkey. For decades he wrestled with the lonely challenge of being a gay man in an environment where such things were not aired. The painter often voiced his commitment to truth, titling his first exhibition *Truth is Beauty and Beauty is God*. Yet the truth of his sexual life was shielded from friends until his mid 40s. He later spoke of his shame over the acts of deception involved.

In this major painting, a fable of Arab origin furnishes a pointed lesson for the closeted artist. Two men encounter a series of judgemental strangers while walking an ass to market. At first, both go on foot and are soon ridiculed for stupidity. If either one mounts the ass, he is berated for selfishness. When both ride, they are condemned for mistreatment. In their desperation to appease all critics, they end up trying to carry their donkey, only to lose it in a nasty accident. In the foreground, the artist observes this narrative unfold from his high vantage point. Now understanding that straining to keep everybody happy pleases no one in the end, he is at last prepared to stand naked before us, in his own truth. It's a 'coming out' announcement from an artist who would make sexuality a central theme in later works.

Lubaina Himid

b.1954 Tanzania, lives UK
We Will Be

1983
Wood, paint, drawing pins,
wool, collage
183 x 91.5
Walker Art Gallery, Liverpool

'We will be / Who we want / Where we want / With whom
we want / In the way that we want / When we want / And
the time is now / And the place is here ...'

Lubaina Himid's verses, inscribed on the wood
cut-out *We Will Be*, ring out like a manifesto – but of
what? They are usually read as an expression of the
artist's black feminism. Himid is recognised as one of
the central figures in Britain's black art scene during
the 1980s – not only for her artistic contributions,
but also as the curator who brought black women
together to mount autonomous group exhibitions.
We Will Be was displayed in the second important
show that Himid organised: *Black Woman Time Now*,
held at London's Battersea Arts Centre in 1983.[42]
With its inscribed text ('the time is now') echoing the
exhibition title, *We Will Be* might seem anchored in
the concerns of that moment. The artwork utters its
rallying cry at the intersection of the feminism that
inspired Himid's collaborations with other women
artists and a black consciousness that fed the black
art movement as a whole.

Identities, however, are complex. *Black Woman
Time Now* included a sizable number of lesbian
women among the fifteen exhibiting artists. As much
as it asserts Himid's determination to break loose at
once from white cultural standards and patriarchal
authority, *We Will Be* serves as a declaration of
liberated sexual desire. Discussion of Himid's art has
often focused on her approach to historical critique –
particularly her exploration of colonialism's legacy via
satirical borrowings from art history. What sometimes
gets overlooked is the way her art has also celebrated
connections between women.[43]

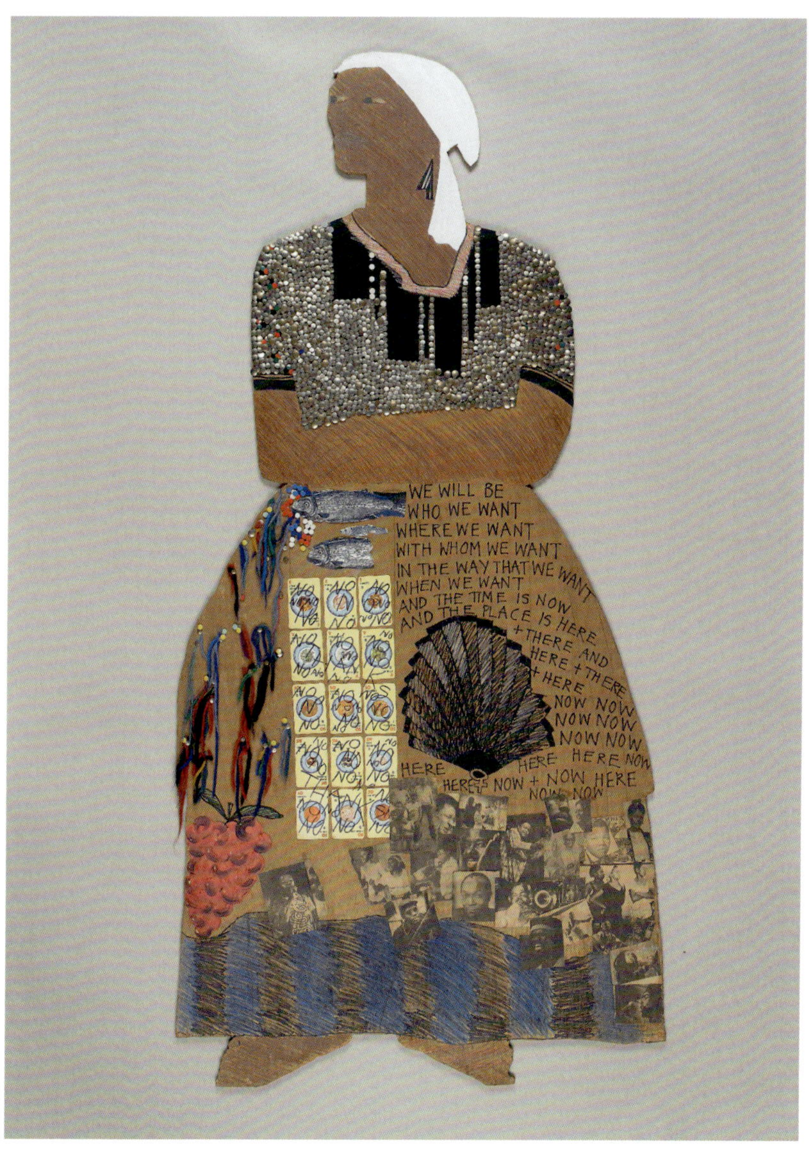

WE WILL BE
WHO WE WANT
WHERE WE WANT
WITH WHOM WE WANT
IN THE WAY THAT WE WANT
WHEN WE WANT
AND THE TIME IS NOW
AND THE PLACE IS HERE.
+ THERE. AND
HERE + THERE
+ HERE
NOW NOW
NOW NOW
NOW NOW
HERE   HERE HERE NOW
HERE   HERE IS NOW + NOW HERE
NOW NOW

Same-sex relationships gained more public visibility in the later decades of the twentieth century, particularly where vocal new movements pushed for lesbian and gay liberation or where laws against homosexuality were repealed. By the late 1960s, David Hockney was painting named same-sex couples.[44] Other queer artists, including Bhupen Khakhar (pp.92–3), made frank, autobiographical works, no longer veiling their experiences of love and sexuality with ambiguity, symbolism or anonymous stand-ins.

Joey Terrill's *Breaking Up/Breaking Down* is a series of twelve scenes that plumb the heartaches of gay relationships with down-to-earth realism. Reproduced opposite is the ex-lover, as pictured in the protagonist's memory. His aviator sunglasses, flannel shirt and moustache are classic elements of the 'clone' street style, popular among American gay men from the mid 1970s. In ensuing scenes, post-break-up, we track the protagonist through stages of grief. He separates his possessions from once-shared kitchen drawers, mourns over a tub of ice cream, embarks on hedonistic nights out in gay clubs, lies awake in the early hours, and is overwhelmed by loss while seeking solace in masturbation.[45]

Terrill's vivid narrative style is clearly inspired by comics. In fact, he later illustrated several issues of a free, health advice comic about safer sex and HIV, aimed at fellow queer Latino men. Unlike Terrill's paintings, the publicly funded *Chicos Modernos* (1989) had to abide by a particularly ugly piece of US law blocking any use of federal money to 'promote, encourage or condone homosexual activities' even in the name of AIDS education efforts.[46] A conservative reaction against the new queer visibility was underway.

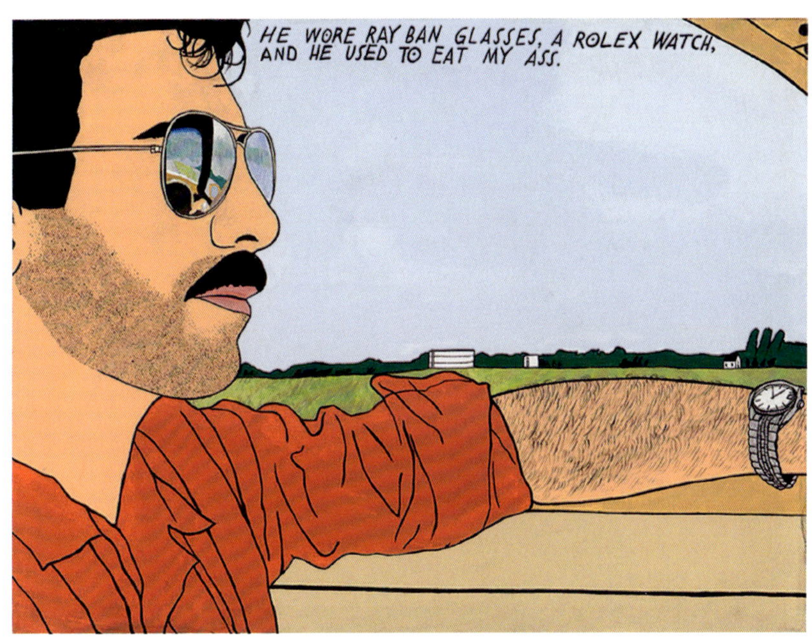

HE WORE RAY BAN GLASSES, A ROLEX WATCH, AND HE USED TO EAT MY ASS.

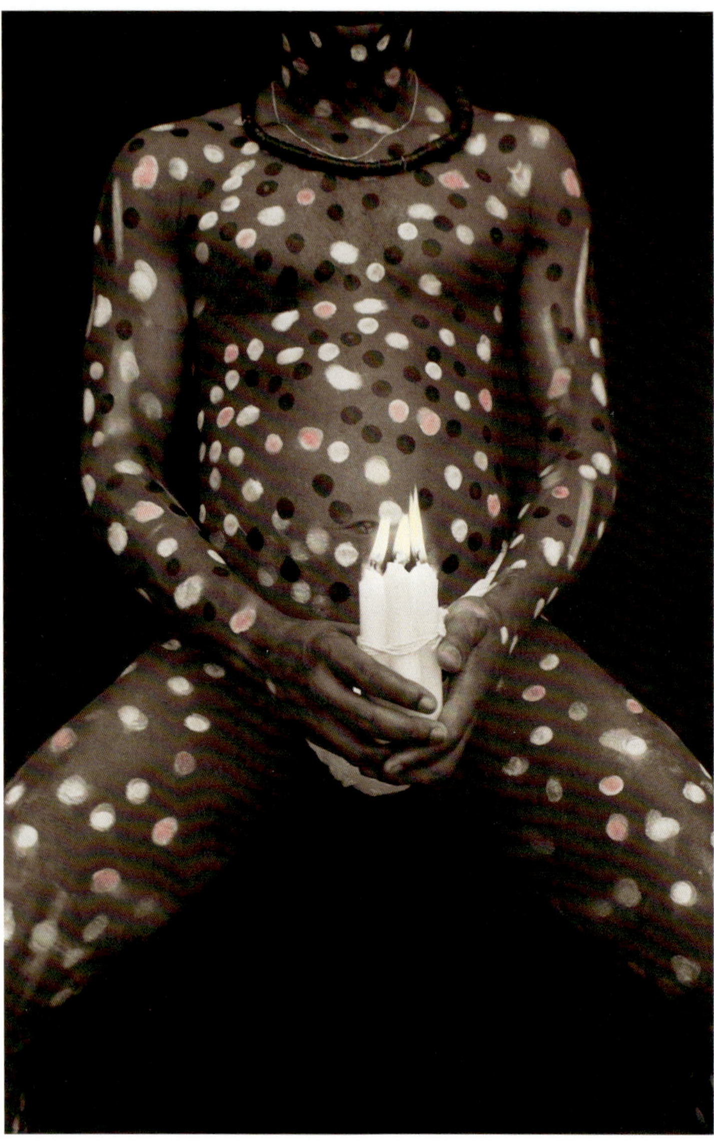

Rotimi Fani-Kayode

b.1955 Nigeria
d.1989 UK
Sonponnoi

1987, printed c.1987–8
Photograph, gelatin silver
print on paper with graphite
and coloured pencil
40.4 x 30.3
Tate. Purchased by the Africa
Acquisitions Committee 2015

Within the Yoruba religion, the smallpox god was at one time powerful, feared and deadly if crossed. Sonponnoi (a name that exists in variant forms such as Sapona) was shunned by his fellow divinities or *orisha*. The god was forced to roam the bush and his shrines were excluded from towns.

But this image was made in Britain, in the late 1980s. The most dreaded disease at that moment was AIDS. As public anxiety around HIV transmission peaked, right-wing groups and tabloid headlines whipped up majority prejudice against both gay men and Africans. Rotimi Fani-Kayode fell into both groups. He was also HIV-positive. The artist found a resonant symbol in the image of an outcast god: one that embodies infection, carrying the threat of death, yet also offers protection. During these painful years, other gay artists were turning to St Sebastian, already an established homoerotic pin-up. Sebastian's old role as plague saint – both protector and sympathetic victim – came back to the fore in queer AIDS-themed art.[47]

It was Sebastian's arrow wounds that suggested to medieval Christians the plague sufferer's pustules. Sonponnoi was also a spotted god. Cult carvings and ritual devotees alike were often covered with dots of paint to evoke the pox's symptoms. During the crisis of the 1980s, the defining sign of AIDS-related illness in the public mind again became a pattern of skin markings: the purplish lesions of Kaposi's sarcoma. All these stigmata seem to merge in *Sonponnoi*. Yet, as the erect candle held by this unwelcome god reminds us, even the disease-bearing queer body feels the flame of desire.

Kiss & Tell
(Susan Stewart,
Persimmon Blackbridge,
Lizard Jones)
Canada
Installation view of
Drawing the Line

1992
Exhibition installation at The
Western Front, Vancouver, BC,
1992 featuring c.100 photographs
Dimensions variable

Drawing the Line was an interactive exhibition devised by lesbian collective Kiss & Tell that toured to fifteen cities. It featured black-and-white images of lesbian sex and intimacy, mostly modelled by Persimmon Blackbridge and Lizard Jones and photographed by Susan Stewart. Ranged across the exhibition walls, the pictures ran from gentle cuddling (clothes on) through explicit images of so-called 'vanilla' sex to scenes involving whips and leather, bondage, simulated violence and, at the extreme end, a man (as voyeur rather than participant). Women were encouraged to write their reactions on the walls – quite literally, to 'draw the line' where they felt images crossed over into problematic territory. (Male visitors were directed to a visitors' book.) Each installation became a battleground in the era's lesbian sex wars.

In the 1980s, fierce disagreements between 'anti-porn' and 'pro-sex' feminists rocked the women's movement in the West. (Variations on the feminist 'sex wars' still rumble, though the pro-sex side of the argument has gained more ground.) Among lesbians, battlefronts took shape around queer sex that employed fetish gear, sex toys or elements of BDSM. As the graffiti from *Drawing the Line* exhibitions demonstrate, the political import of such practices and related erotic imagery often became flash points.[48] What some visitors welcomed as an overdue celebration of kinky lesbian desire, others saw as tired male objectification of women, irresponsibly repackaged. Gleeful comments from S&M dykes butted up against sobering reflections from rape survivors. It is for inviting these raw debates on to the walls of an art gallery – more than for Kiss & Tell's photographs – that *Drawing the Line* is remembered as one of the most effective examples of queer exhibition-making.

BEAUTIFUL

+feels good

I LOVE THIS

bondage

GREAT:
WE ARE
GOING TO DO
TO OURSELVES
WHAT MYSOGINIST
WANT TO CONTINUE
TO ACT OUT MALE
VIOLENCE TO PUT OUR

you can open yourself
by closing off senses —
safely, consensually

sweet baby

NICE TO SEE
SOMEONE
TRYING
IT
OUT!

hey! hey!
ho! ho!
this co-ed thing
has got to go

HE ALSO LIKES
BATMAN.

what is he doing with
I think he's
got a HARD-on

up yours!

HATE IT!

I saw the
line with the
rope around
the neck.
Too easy
to die.

not find
place
lie down?
reminds me
high school.
my
gh school!!

K, BUT
LIKE TO
THE
EYES

J A P A N E S E   B U L L S H I T   A R T   M A G A Z I N E

I'm gonna
tell my
mom!

Rrrrggg!

sorry
i'm all
tied up at
the moment

Whole magazines
full of this at
Frenchy's k&t on
Turk St. Pretty
traditional male
oriented stuff.

Not so
male

NO   BULLSHIT   NO   NO NICE MACRAME!   NO   NO

This is pure yuck to me, as a survivor of ritualized abuse.

TRUSSED
All DRESSED UP
AND NO PLACE
TO GO...?
— like MADONNA?

Symbolic Oppression

WOULD LOVE TO BE IN HER PLACE

I PREFER ENDORPHINS

Beautiful Bondage

ONE OF THE FEW/ONLY
WOMEN OF COLOR IN THIS
EXHIBIT IS TIED UP —
MAYBE JUST A COINCIDENCE?

BEYOND LIT CANDLES
KNIVES & ROPE ARE
THEY SURE
WORSE!

TOO VULNERABLE!
WHERE'S PARTNER?

why isn't he off?
jerking like

I don't want to
have sex with
some asshole
watchi

Agony is
only worth
it FOR THE
ECSTASY

P.S. THE ROPE AROUND
THE NECK IS
TOTALLY LOOSE,
KIDS, DON'T PANIC

it is a matter of
excitement not mutilation

ropes are
- too loose
- too nice

MAYBE I WA

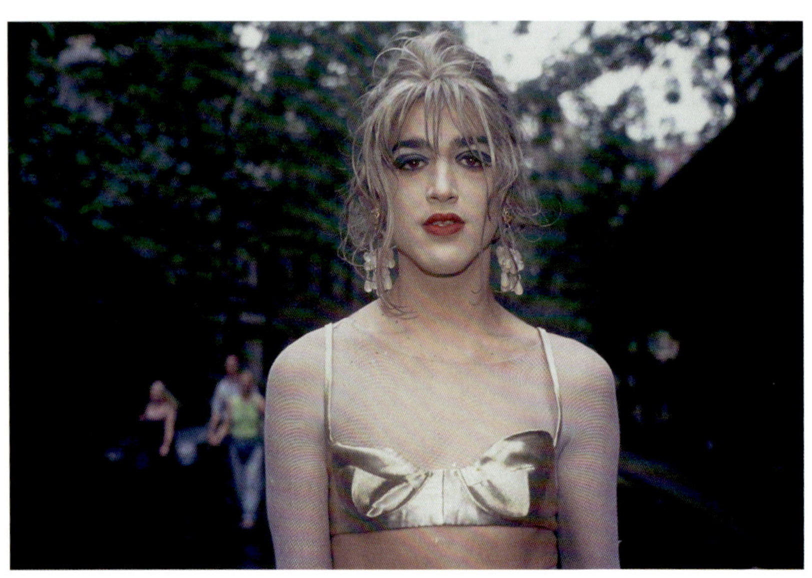

Nan Goldin

b.1953 USA

*Jimmy Paulette after
the parade, NYC, 1991*

1991
Photograph, colour,
Cibachrome print, on paper
38.9 x 59.4
Tate. Presented by the American
Fund for the Tate Gallery,
courtesy of Peter Norton 2012

This photograph is one of several Nan Goldin made of three drag-queen friends on the day of New York's Pride parade. The pictures are not presented as a series, but a chronological sequence can be traced. Initial scenes show Tabboo!, Misty and Jimmy Paulette dressing; street photographs document the parade; later, the tired queens grab a taxi and unwind at home. The images became widely known thanks to their central position in *The Other Side*, a photo book Goldin issued two years later (Jimmy Paulette featuring on the cover).

Pride parades – a defining symbol of the LGBT liberation movement – are held in ever more cities around the world each year. The model for all subsequent parades was that held in June 1970, on the first anniversary of New York's Stonewall uprising. Goldin was still a teenager at the time and living in Boston. Two years later, she began taking the earliest pictures that would go on to appear in *The Other Side*: black-and-white photos of friends and roommates who were trans women, drag queens or gender fluid. The Other Side was a drag bar where Goldin often snapped her Boston friends in full beauty-pageant glory.

My own first taste of Pride was in 1991, on this same Saturday in late June. Jimmy Paulette certainly had the more fabulous outfit, but in London, we had sunshine. It rained on New York's parade floats that day and Jimmy Paulette looks a little bedraggled as she faces Goldin's camera.[49] The level of trust between artist and subject demonstrated in this seemingly off-guard image is perhaps the core characteristic of Goldin's photography.

Glenn Ligon
b.1960 USA
*Notes on the Margin
of the Black Book*

1991–3
91 offset prints, framed:
27.9 x 28.6 each; 78 text pages,
framed: 13.3 x 18.4 each
Solomon R. Guggenheim Museum,
New York

Born of an era when fashionable academics loved to 'deconstruct' and 'reframe' their topics of study, Glenn Ligon's *Notes on the Margin of the Black Book* applies both operations, quite literally, to the photographic work of Robert Mapplethorpe (1946–89). Ligon dismantled the 1986 photo book – a collection of homoerotic photographs of black men – and presented its ninety-one illustrations in separate frames. Yet the critical 'reframing' of Mapplethorpe's imagery is effected through seventy-eight quotations hung between the photographs.

Mapplethorpe's work with black models drew ambivalent responses from black gay viewers. There are few other images in art that take such queer delight in the physical beauty of black men. Yet this white photographer's pursuit of formal perfection involved marshalling black bodies into strict compositions. In the context of a long history of white people's exploitation, control and objectification of black people's bodies, Mapplethorpe's single-minded art was troubling. Several pictures in *The Black Book* even appear to flirt with such racist stereotypes as the mythically large black penis. The book provoked anger on publication. *Notes on the Margin* samples those critical black responses, the quotations drawing on well-known writers, men Ligon had interviewed in bars, and the artist's own reflections.

The debate over Mapplethorpe took a dramatic turn after his death in 1989. As politicians railed against his explicit images of New York's gay leather scene, Mapplethorpe's touring retrospective was cancelled in Washington and sparked an obscenity trial in Cincinnati. A stirred-up US Congress now barred federal arts money from supporting work on gay themes. In the wake of this moral panic, Mapplethorpe's queer critics reassessed their loyalties. Ligon's installation documents the still recent homophobic outcry, producing a complex artwork that neither condemns nor exonerates Mapplethorpe.

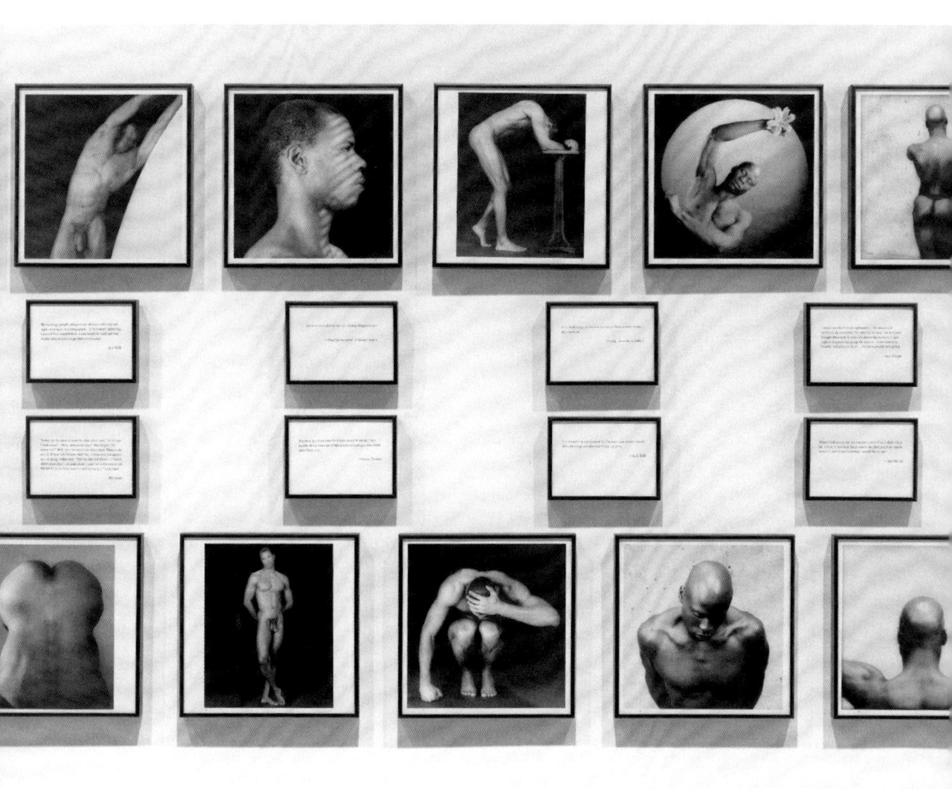

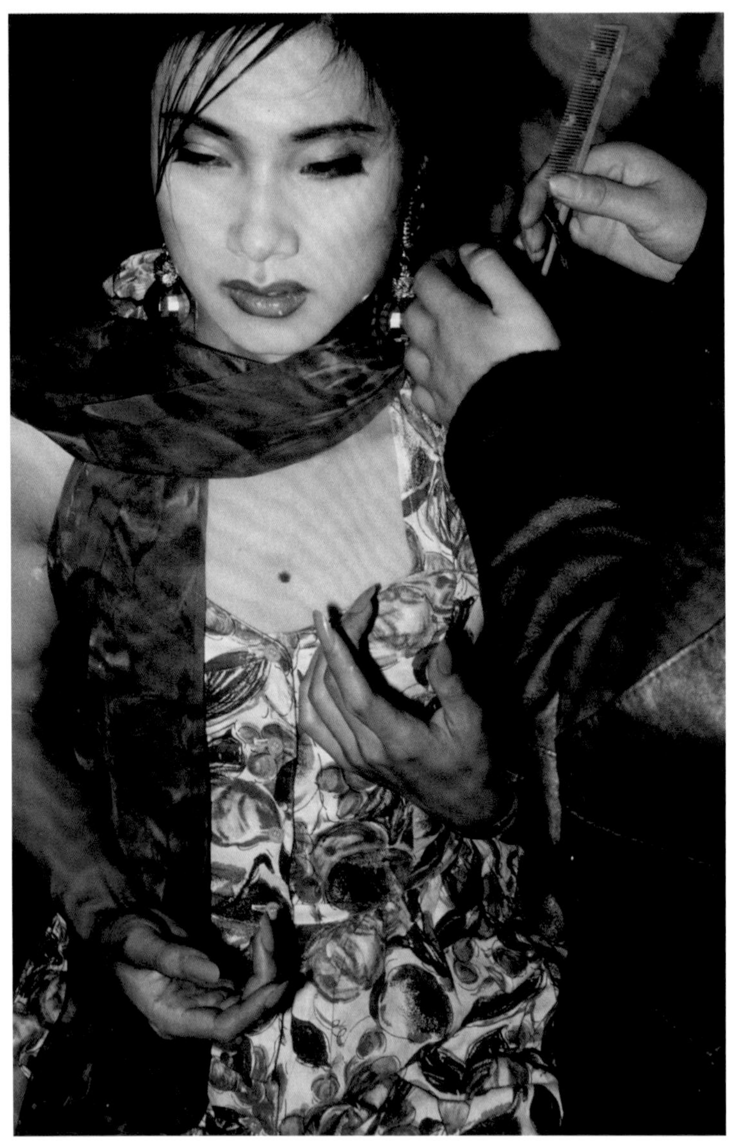

Ma Liuming

b.1969 China

Fen · Ma Liuming

1993
Photograph, gelatin silver
print on paper
61 x 50.8
Tate. Purchased with funds
provided by the Asia Pacific
Acquisitions Committee 2016

In 1993, the year he helped establish the avant-garde artist community soon known as Beijing East Village, Ma Liuming was a young painter in search of an expressive language. The story goes that a drunken clothes-swap revealed how readily Ma achieved the semblance of a beautiful woman. Over the next eleven years, he explored this gift via a partially feminine alter ego, Fen Ma Liuming.

Ma avoided constructing a unified gender for his performance persona. Fen Ma Liuming embodies a gender patchwork; her face is female and his body is male. In Taoist terms, the character's face expresses the feminine yin principle, the body the masculine yang. Fen Ma Liuming emphasised these distinct aspects by performing naked.

This photograph records Fen Ma Liuming's debut before an intimate crowd of East Village friends. A make-up artist applies final touches to the character, who wears a sleeveless dress. Later in this performance, Fen Ma Liuming stripped naked, masturbated to orgasm and then drank the semen mixed with water. While this may seem like the ultimate demonstration of the character's male aspect, the loss of semen with its store of *jing* (vital essence) is traditionally believed to weaken male yang. Consuming the *jing*-rich semen, Fen Ma Liuming's yin aspect completes the cycle. Such forms of art making were viewed as deeply transgressive by Chinese authorities at the time. The following year, Ma Liuming was arrested during another naked performance and imprisoned for two months on charges of pornographic offences. Further raids and forced evictions brought a swift end to the East Village experiment.

Tracey Moffatt
b.1960 Australia
Doll Birth, 1972

1994
From *Scarred for Life*
Lithograph on paper
80 × 60
Tate. Purchased 1998

How many of us could disclose tales of such experiences: seemingly harmless, briefly divine, and terminated abruptly by a stony voice of disapproval? When young, we feel out the boundaries of permissible self-expression, sometimes learning that particular forms of fun breach hallowed rules. Such lessons commonly befall children who transgress the gender borderlines. The hapless kid who is disciplined for dressing up in the 'wrong' clothes, playing the 'wrong' games, or for innocently voicing an 'inappropriate' ambition is a stock character in queer life narratives.

Scarred for Life is a series of blow-ups of simulated magazine pages: an exposé of suburban childhood trauma. The nine scenarios in Moffatt's carefully staged photographs range from quietly harrowing to darkly comic. In *Doll Birth, 1972*, two boys aged around eight or nine are disturbed at the climax of their game. The boy playing midwife looks up nervously – his friend still deeply immersed in a dazzling performance of childbirth. The caption supplies the denouement: 'His mother caught him giving birth to a doll. He was banned from playing with the boy next door again.' It might be a line from a kooky, independent film comedy. But underneath the humour, Moffatt's tender direction of her young actors – the artist, incidentally, is also a filmmaker – elicits our empathy. The sad truth is that many a queer life has been scarred by just such barbs, inflicted by elders convinced they were setting things right.

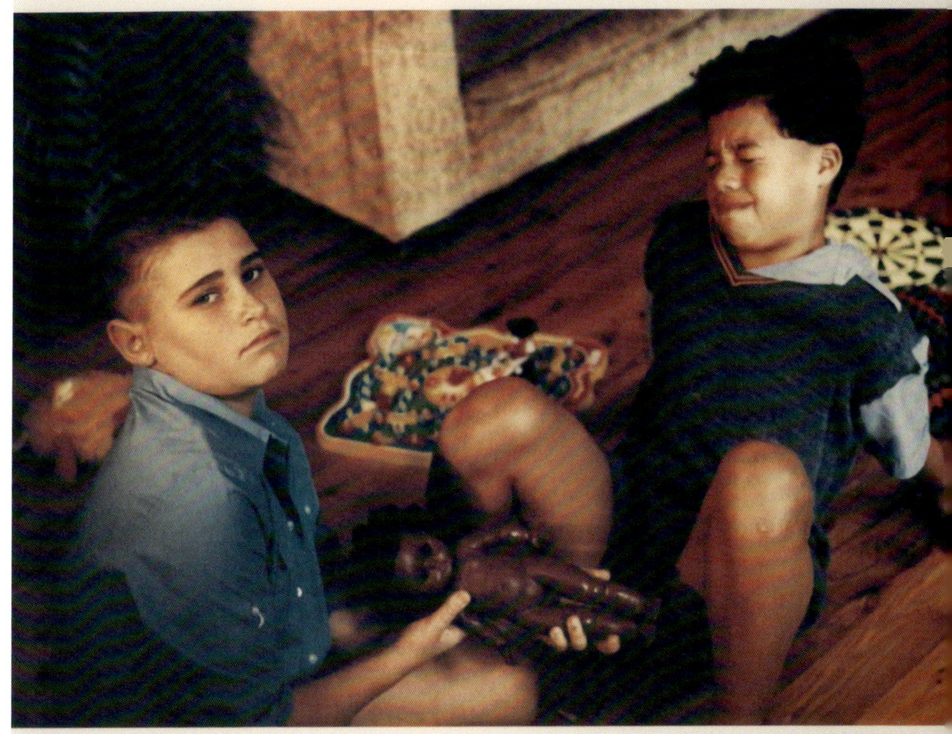

Tracey Moffatt

Doll Birth, 1972 His mother caught him giving birth to a doll.
He was banned from playing with the boy
next door again.

Wolfgang Tillmans
b.1968 Germany
Jochen taking a bath

1997
From *if one thing matters,
everything matters, installation
room 2, 1995–1997*
Digital print on paper
40.6 x 30.4
Tate. Presented by Tate Patrons
2007

if one thing matters, everything matters. The title of Wolfgang Tillmans' 2003 exhibition at Tate Britain challenged the ingrained biases that rank some things as inherently unimportant.[50] For this contemplative artist, a crumpled trouser leg drying on a radiator and the scum on the surface of a cup of coffee are visual experiences to be treasured – equally worthy of careful documentation as a world-famous supermodel.[51]

Yet, it's hard to escape the feeling that certain things matter just that bit more. In the second room at Tate's show, Tillmans installed a selection of photographs spanning the period of his relationship with fellow German artist Jochen Klein (the whole set is now in Tate's collection). *Jochen taking a bath* was blown-up to giant poster size, hinting that this tender domestic scene was an unofficial centrepiece. From remarks Tillmans made in an interview a year earlier, it's clear that other works in the selection related to moments shared with Klein.[52] Most direct is an image of their fingers, clasped against hospital bed sheets, taken on the final day of Klein's AIDS-related illness. Titled *Für Immer Burgen* 1997, it's heart-rending. The photographs Tillmans arranged on the walls between these emotive poles take on quiet significance. Is that the couple, gazing at the moonrise on holiday? Are those Jochen's trousers? Did they share that breakfast during the days of Klein's illness?[53] Tillmans has resisted biographical readings of his work. Nevertheless, it's hard not to think that for one summer in 2003, two walls in Tate Britain became a memorial to queer love and loss.

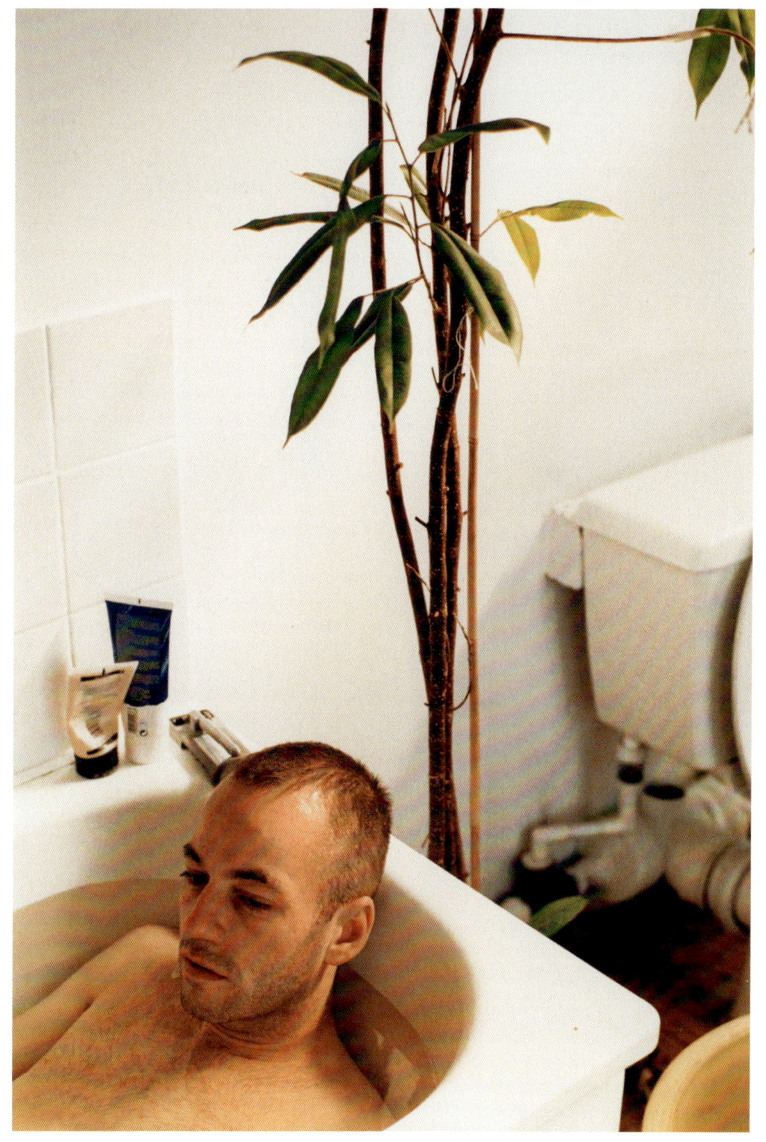

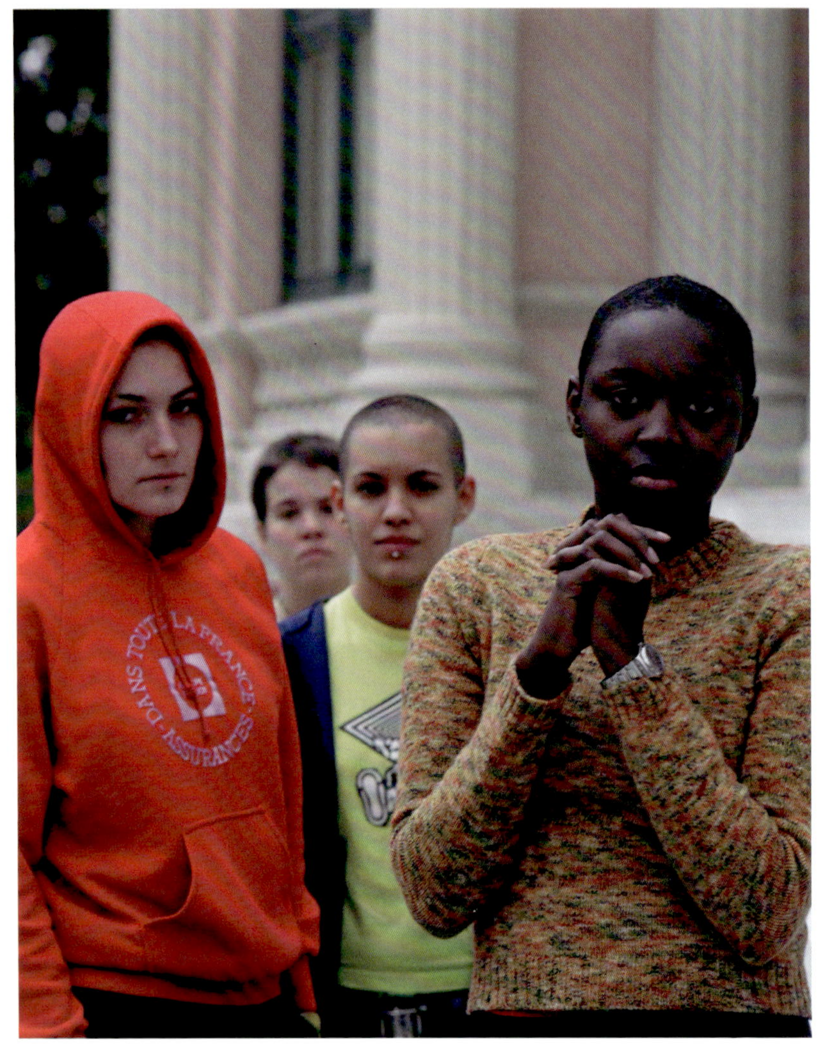

Carmela García

b.1964 Spain
Untitled

1999, printed 2000
From the series, *Chicas, deseos y
ficción* ('Girls, Desires and Fiction')
Chromogenic print on paper
mounted on aluminium
149.7 x 119
Museo Nacional Centro de Arte
Reina Sofía, Madrid

The photographs and film segments that make up
Carmela García's *Chicas, deseos y ficción* portray
a lesbian-centred world very different from the
everyday. This is not a cramped bar or a forest retreat,
but a whole city full of confident, desiring, queer
women. They check out other women at newsstands,
flirt in doorways, cruise on park walks and follow
each other home. Every encounter is suddenly rich
with possibilities.

What we are viewing is a fiction, as the series title
reminds us. The artist and her accomplices staged
these scenes around Madrid; the one reproduced here
was shot in Buen Retiro Park. It's not just the men and
straight women who vanish from García's reimagined
city; children, teenagers, anyone much above thirty-
five also seem curiously absent. One might hesitate
to describe this as a lesbian utopia – many gay women
would jump on the first train out of Garcíaville – but
this visual experiment does encourage us to reflect
critically on the spaces we move through every day.

In real cities, many are all too practised at
anticipating hostility and prejudice from strangers.
What would it take for those currently most
marginalised to experience the public realm as fully
theirs by right, with the same degree of security and
freedom enjoyed by society's most privileged? García's
alternative Madrid enables one marginal group to
weigh the implications of that (authentically utopian)
prospect. One image shows two women kissing,
carefree, in a sunlit street and, for a pleasant change,
the only attention they attract is from a fellow dyke,
looking wistfully over her shoulder as she passes.

Mrinalini Mukherjee
1949–2015 India
Jauba

2000
Hemp fibre and steel
143 x 133 x 110
Tate. Presented by
Amrita Jhaveri 2013

Only child to a sculptor and a painter, Mrinalini Mukherjee didn't lack encouragement as an aspiring artist. In her early career, however, she met with condescension from many in India's art scene, her chosen medium of hand-knotted plant fibres disparaged as a form of craft.

Initially wall-based, Mukherjee's artworks had evolved into freestanding sculptures by the 1980s. Occasionally, they sprouted limbs to assume a clearly anthropomorphic presence. Yet the majority of her fibre sculptures are more ambiguously biomorphic – in keeping with her unplanned approach to their making. Generally symmetrical about a vertical axis, many reveal one or more central orifices surrounded by hoods, flaps and undulating folds. Although Mukherjee never adheres to real-world anatomy, the association with vulvas is inescapable in such works as *Yakshi* (1984), *Yogini* (1986), *Pushp* (1993), *Aranyani* (1996) and *Jauba*. The opulent excess of their creases and openings, realised on an imposing scale, only serves to make them more magnificently sexual.

Western art proffers its own examples of women who explored vaginal or specifically labial forms: whether the faint hints that some discern in the work of Barbara Hepworth (1903–75) and Georgia O'Keeffe (1887–1986) or the open references in the feminist art of Judy Chicago (b.1939). But those widely cited examples might seem icily clinical against Mukherjee's wonderfully malleable sculptures. Her soft, organic materials, dyed in warm reds and maroons, pay a more apt tribute to the female body. Mukherjee, like most artists, kept very quiet about inspirations and personal feelings alike. Speculation is, however, superfluous. These giant, lovingly fashioned monuments to the central locus of women's sexual pleasure are the legacy of a queer art of devotion.

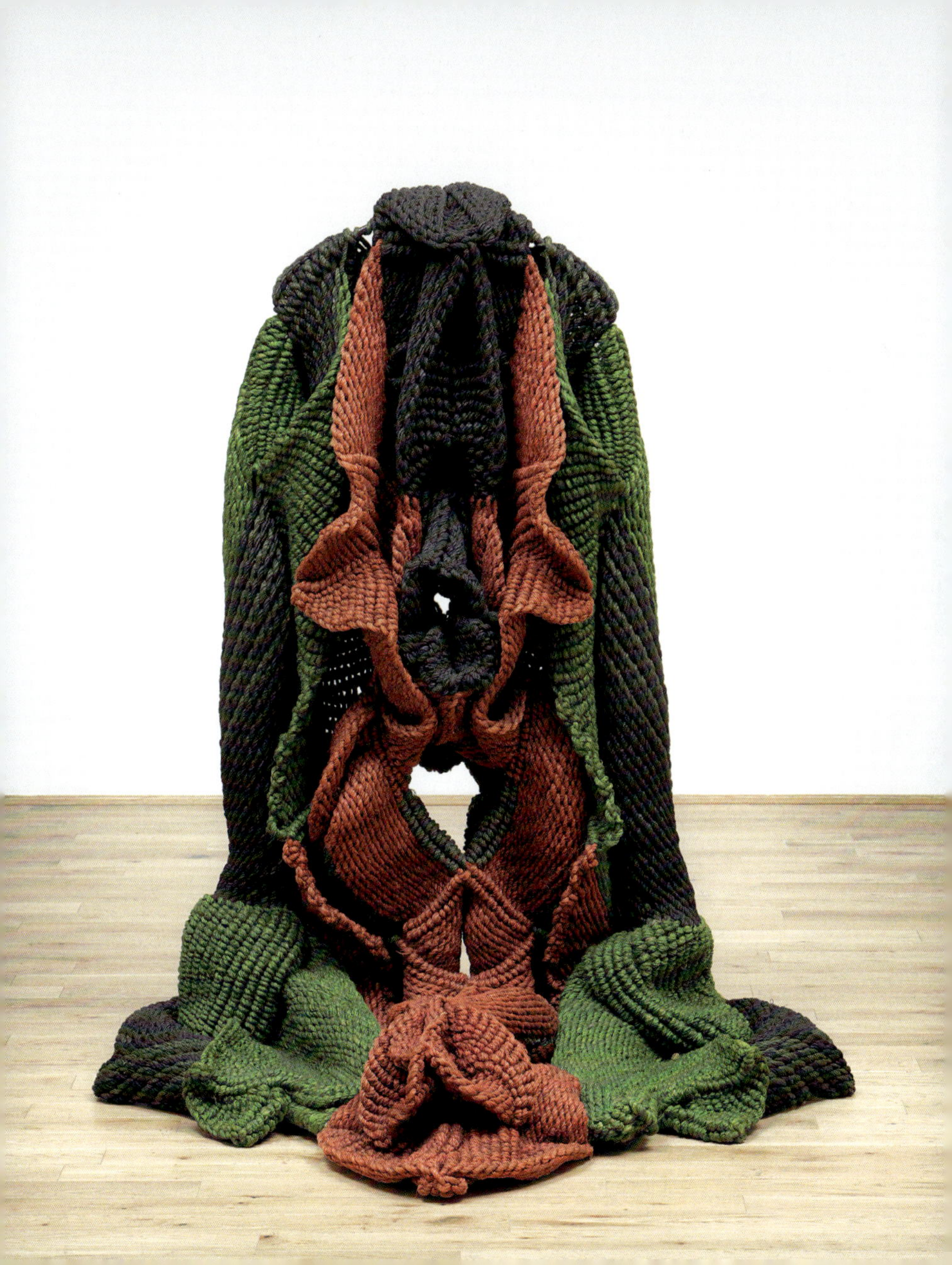

Zanele Muholi

b.1972 South Africa
ID Crisis

2003
Photograph, gelatin silver
print on paper
35.3 x 48
Tate. Purchased with funds
provided by Wendy Fisher 2015

In the bright morning light, a figure dresses in a humble room. Wearing men's shorts, a fraying bandage in hand, the figure is caught halfway through the action of breast binding. We recognise a person who routinely presents a masculine identity to the world, but cannot read whether this individual identifies as a man, as a butch woman, or has a different or shifting gender identity.[54] That open-ended range of possibility is one aspect of what makes this such an affecting queer image.

The artist, Zanele Muholi, is a queer visual activist who uses photography as a means of countering homophobia and transphobia. The hundreds of powerful and beautiful images produced in the process have earned Muholi appreciation and awards around the world, and it seems odd to be speaking already of *ID Crisis* as an 'early' work. Yet this image dates from the end of a surprisingly recent formal training. (Before her artistic career, Muholi had already worked as a journalist, human-rights activist and hair stylist.)

At the time of this work, the participants in Muholi's photographs are not named and their faces are frequently turned away or out of shot. The artist's camera pinpoints telling details: hair on a transgender body (*Bra*); a scar left by a knife wound (*Aftermath*); a butch woman's outfit (*In-security*); a bath that may follow a 'curative' rape (*Ordeal*).[55] All invite us to think more deeply about the conditions in which queer black identities are lived in contemporary South Africa, where formal legal equality does little to mitigate the threat of violent – and often deadly – hate crimes.

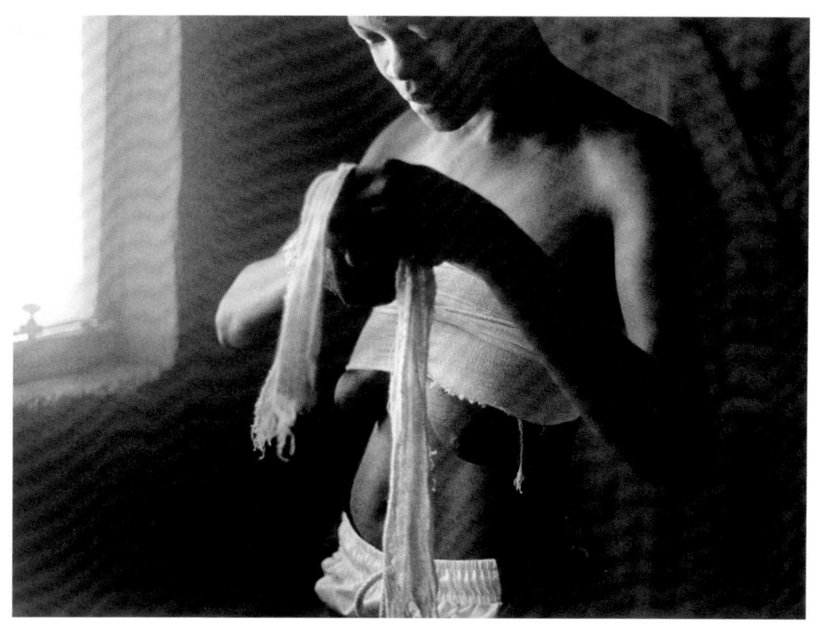

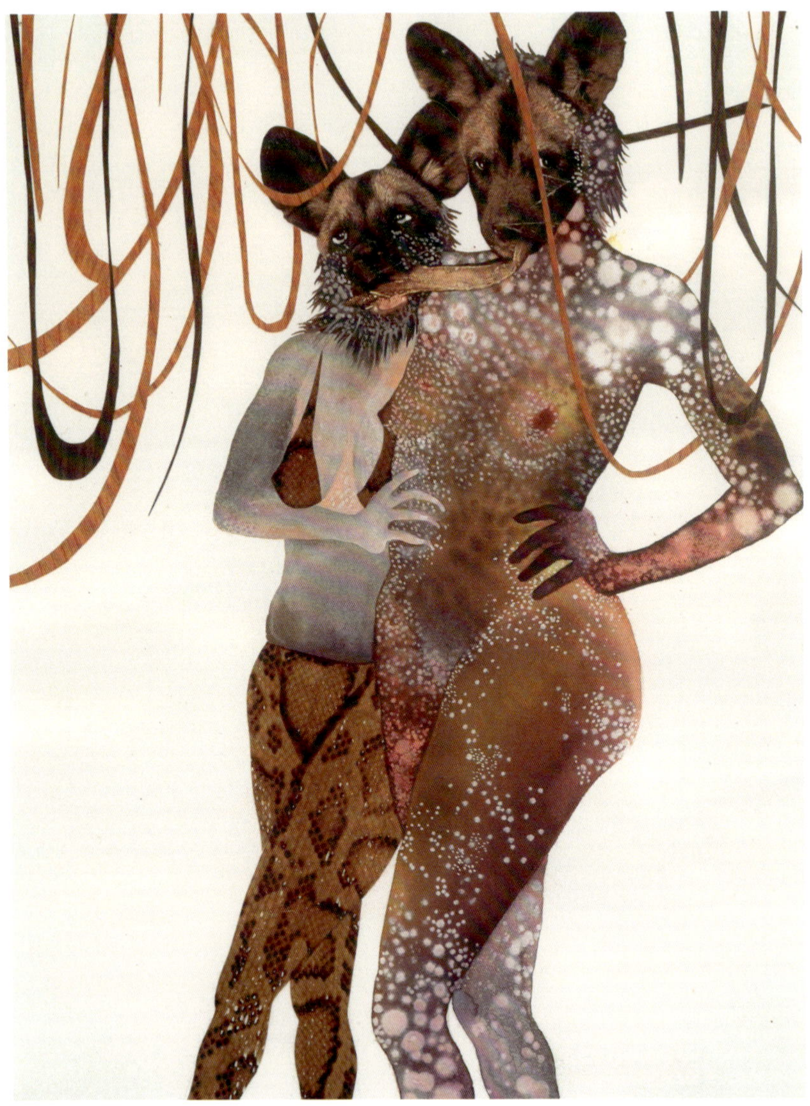

Wangechi Mutu

b.1972 Kenya, lives USA
Intertwined

2003
Collage and watercolour
on paper
40.6 x 30.5
Collection Susanne Vielmetter,
Los Angeles

The sleek muzzles on this pair are those of African wild dogs, notoriously efficient hunters. While fearsome killers, wild dogs are also beautiful, long-limbed athletes whose dappled pelts justify the rival species name, painted hunting dogs. It's a label suggestive of something not entirely real: an artistic fiction of the natural world. And that's before Wangechi Mutu combined those canine heads with humanoid bodies, sourced from fashion photographs.

In her two-dimensional works, Mutu typically combines an impressive range of media – refined collage techniques melding with gorgeously hand-painted surfaces. Relatively modest in size and materials, *Intertwined* is still representative in its unsettling elegance. Mutu pieces together wildly disparate bodily components: human, animal, vegetable, mechanical – even extra-terrestial. Even if some collaged elements are male in origin, the end products are unmistakeably feminine. Her creations are seductively beautiful, in spite (or because) of the livid spots of colour that bloom upon mottled skin like microbial cultures in a petri dish. Far from ailing, Mutu's hybrids appear vivacious and agile: a blend of cyborg, goddess and supermodel.

Perhaps 'femme' would be a more fitting descriptor than 'feminine'. The unquestionable glamour of these beings is of the fierce kind. In common with other superhuman types in this book – in works by Glyn Philpot (pp.44–5), James Richmond Barthé (pp.62–3), Chitra Ganesh (pp.126–7), and Allyson Mitchell (pp.132–3) – Mutu's figures transgress boundaries of socially approved behaviour for their gender. The queerness of Mutu's creatures merely becomes more apparent when – as here, in *Intertwined* – desire flourishes between these femmes.

Henrik Olesen
b.1967 Denmark,
lives Germany
Untitled (x 3)

2004
Each image: 32 digital prints
on paper
From top to bottom:
111 x 155.5
110.5 x 155.5
107.7 x 151.4
Tate. Purchased with funds
provided by the 2004 Outset
Frieze Acquisitions Fund for
Tate 2004

If there were an award for the most innocuous cliché in the language, 'it's a nice day to be out' would make the shortlist. The remark makes up for its banality by reminding the hearer that, *Yes, it is a nice day.* It's no mystery if this sunny commonplace was co-opted as a blithe celebration of LGBT pride and visibility.[56] In the topmost print shown here, the underlying graffiti inscription uses the expression in that sense. An aggressive, homophobic counter-inscription forms a secondary layer. The diagonal stroke cancels the initial meaning and the word 'shot' has been interpolated to twist the message into a menacing expression of hate.

These three *Untitled* prints are part of a series of artworks that Henrik Olesen made using photographs of homophobic graffiti appropriated from websites. The other two graffiti messages we see here read 'ALL FAGETS in the Army Will Be Killed' and 'Roy is HOMO'. The artist made a unique print of each image at a vastly enlarged scale, using sticky tape to tile sheets of regular printer stationery into a grid. When displayed, they are simply attached to the wall, unframed. Olesen has made further artworks that relate to gay history or that highlight the current legal prohibitions of homosexuality around the world, often using similarly modest means.

With their tacky materials and low-resolution digital images, their clumsy photography, crudely scrawled graffiti and angry homophobia, Olesen's prints are ugly on many levels. Within the context of an art gallery – traditionally dedicated to beauty and lofty sentiments – they make an unseemly intrusion. Olesen reminds the viewer that a reservoir of hatred towards anyone queer still permeates our daily environment, on both sides of those pristine white walls.

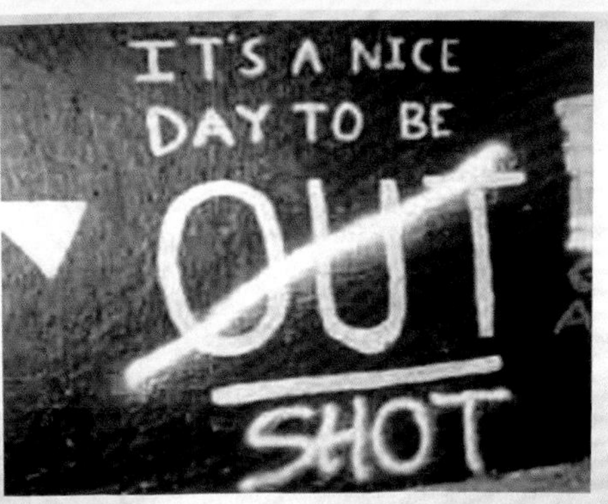
IT'S A NICE
DAY TO BE
OUT
SHOT

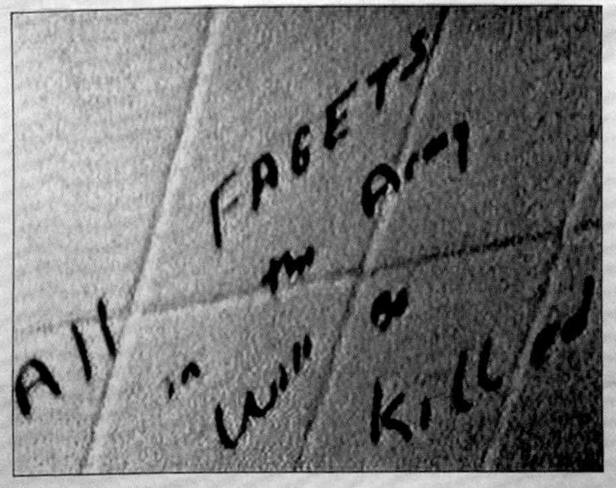
All FAGETS
in the Army
will be
killed

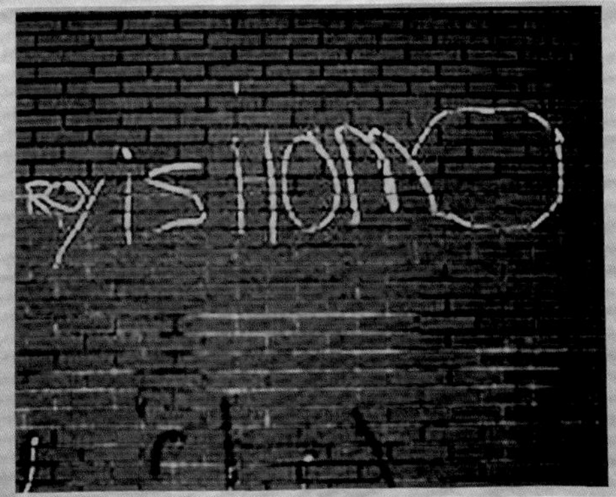
ROY IS HOMO

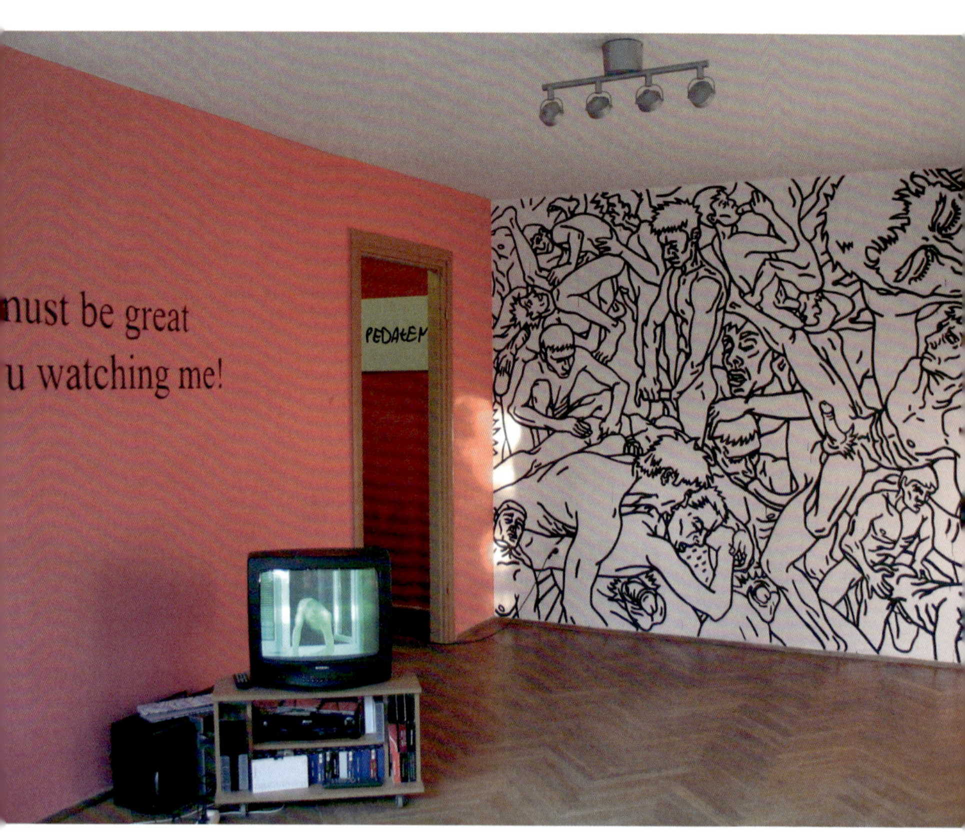
must be great
u watching me!
PEDAŁEM

Karol Radziszewski
b.1980 Poland
Fags
Pedały

2005
Temporary installation

Visitors entering Karol Radziszewski's solo exhibition in Warsaw in 2005 were greeted by the blunt message, 'I am a fag' (*Jestem pedałem*).[57] This proclamation, scrawled in black paint on a white canvas, set the tone for what Radziszewski describes as 'the first openly homosexual exhibition in Poland'.[58] Titled simply *Fags*, the show included works produced over a three-year period. The main space was dominated by a mural: black outlines defining a forest of naked, humping 'fags' across one full wall.

Fags was staged in a private apartment rather than a gallery. Given the widespread homophobia in Poland at that time, it's tempting to put this DIY approach down to necessity. The work of getting queer art seen often involves bypassing gatekeepers of the established art world. Yet, Radziszewski and his curator collaborator, Marcin Różyc, insisted theirs was a voluntary gesture. They linked *Fags* to the tradition of queer cultural expression in private salons and to a lineage of Polish artists exhibiting in domestic spaces, going back at least to the 1970s.[59]

With a centrepiece that might have been lifted from a pornographic colouring book, *Fags* dared visitors to dismiss Radziszewski's work on grounds of taste. The artist's aim was perhaps to defuse homophobic stereotypes – here, of gay hypersexuality – by making them ridiculously literal (bright pink walls elsewhere in the installation being another hint). It's a ploy Radziszewski revisited. *Fag Fighters* (2007) used video to construct a fictional queer gang in pink balaclavas, who subject male victims to drunken acts of sexual violence. The gay bogeymen that stalk some homophobic imaginations are played out in *Fag Fighters* to the point of absurdity.

Chi Peng
b.1981 China
I Fuck Me: Office

2005
Colour photograph
120 x 155
M97 Gallery, Shanghai

In the year he graduated from Beijing's Central Academy of Fine Arts, Chi Peng made a series of large-format photographs where he takes part in sexual encounters with a digitally collaged double. *I Fuck Me* was less a provocative debut as confirmation of Chi's willingness to explore queer visual territory in his meticulously manipulated images – already being exhibited internationally a year earlier. In his *Consubstantiality* series (2003), for example, Chi had stitched differently sexed bodies into nude composites, using his own body as the base.

The sex in *I Fuck Me* takes place in awkward, exposed locations: a telephone booth, a public toilet cubicle or under the desk of an open-plan office. Like the movie cliché of kitchen-table sex, the uncomfortable settings suggest desire at its most urgent, or else a sublime indifference to social sanctions. In a contrasting second series with the same title, the two Chi Pengs fuck in dimly lit seclusion. Yet now, the artist's selves shoot anxious glances over shoulders in some scenes, as if fearful of being discovered.

Critics often highlight narcissism as a theme in these works, but this possibly misrepresents painstaking artistic constructions as acts of personal disclosure. Chi's simulated self-love may well be partly tactical, the sheer tricksiness of *I Fuck Me* helping to secure art-world approval. That both figures always remain amusingly recognisable as Chi proves beyond doubt that these images are digital fictions and not documents of alarmingly real gay sex. Directly affirming queer desire, only to disavow it on closer inspection, *I Fuck Me* received successful gallery exposure in China and the West.

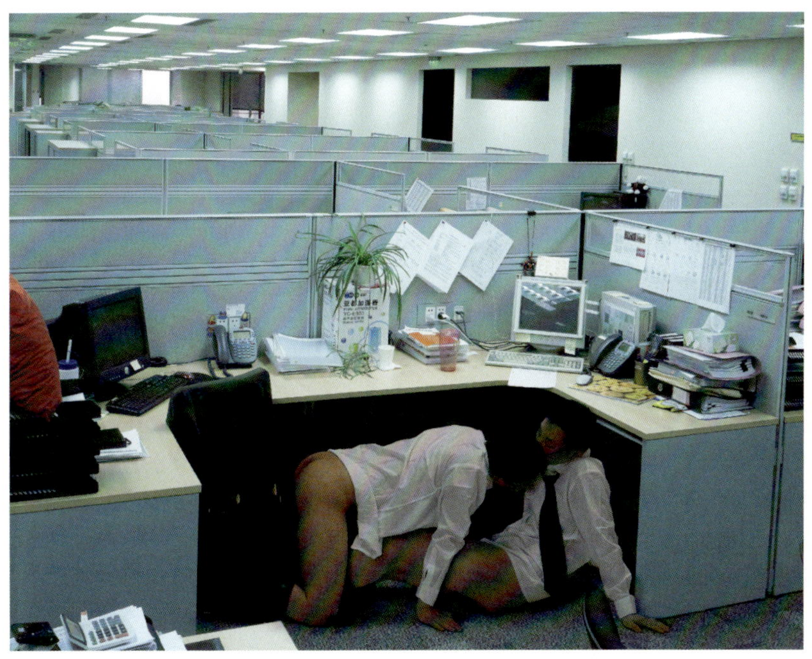

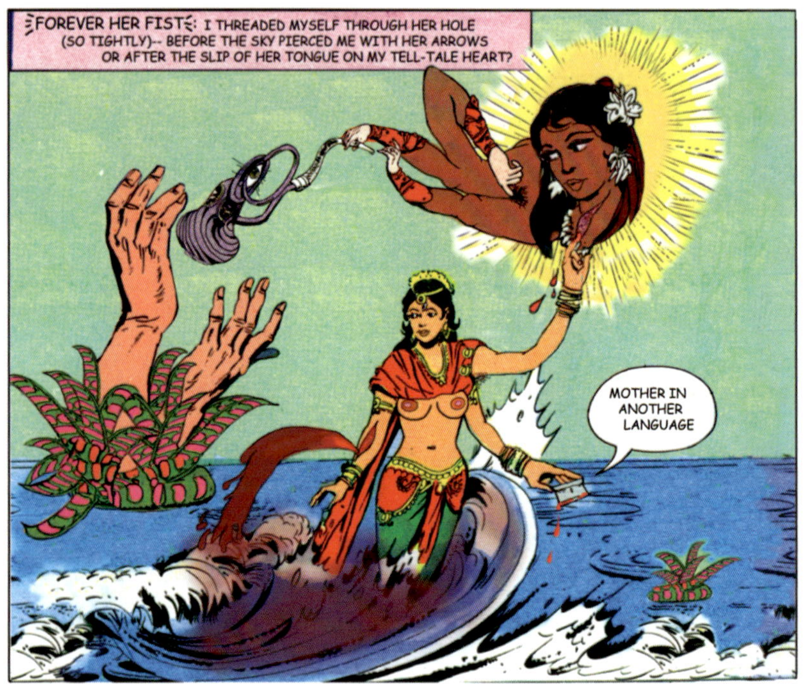
FOREVER HER FIST: I THREADED MYSELF THROUGH HER HOLE (SO TIGHTLY)-- BEFORE THE SKY PIERCED ME WITH HER ARROWS OR AFTER THE SLIP OF HER TONGUE ON MY TELL-TALE HEART?
MOTHER IN ANOTHER LANGUAGE

Chitra Ganesh

b.1975 USA

Forever Her Fist

2006
Digital print on paper
pasted on board
48.3 x 58.4
Private collection

Forever Her Fist; with three small words, Chitra Ganesh catapults us into a higher plane of unbridled queer desires. If we let that paean to feminine penetration sink in, we may well find ourselves floating in the company of her triple-armed sky goddess. Those limbs of hers, however, are deceptive. What looked for a moment like one of several hairy armpits begins to suggest a divine groin, where one of this being's many digits is firmly lodged. It's a demonstration of superhuman self-pleasuring.

Forget any glancing echoes of 1960s pop art; Ganesh is playing a very different game with her appropriated vintage comic book material.[60] Think back to the subversive photomontage creations of Hannah Höch (pp.52–3) and you'll be on the right track. The incongruous collision of body parts resembles examples of exquisite corpse: the surrealists' favourite drawing game, in which players take turns adding parts to an unseen body. Ganesh uses another tactic beloved of the surrealists, automatic writing, to compose wording unconstrained by everyday narrative logic. Here, those free-flowing words press against keenly felt erogenous zones, while conveying disturbing hints of violence. Being pierced by arrows may be an age-old metaphor for erotic surrender, but one that threatens to kill. The 'slip of her tongue on my tell-tale heart' may set pulses a-flutter, but invokes a macabre story by Edgar Allan Poe (1809–49). Look below and you'll notice the regal central figure is rising from a seething bath of her own blood, gushing from a long wound in one of her three arms. By unseating normative expectations of anatomy, gravity, pain and pleasure, Ganesh invites us to rethink our own physical and sexual boundaries.

Akram Zaatari
b.1966 Lebanon
Objects of Study/
The Archive of Studio
Shehrazade/Hashem el
Madani/Studio Practices

2007
117 photographs, gelatin silver
prints on paper
Illustrated (clockwise from
top left):

Bashasha (left) and a friend. Studio
Shehrazade, Saida, Lebanon, late
1950s. Hashem el Madani
19.1 x 28.9

Tarho and El Masri. Studio
Shehrazade, Saida, Lebanon, 1958.
Hashem el Madani
19 x 28.9

Amin Hijazi (left) and his cousin
Gharamti. Studio Shehrazade,
Saida, Lebanon, 1950s–1960s.
Hashem el Madani
19 x 28.9

Ahmad el Abed, and his friend
Rajab Arna'out. Madani's parents'
home, the studio, Saida, Lebanon,
1948–53. Hashem el Madani
19 x 28.9

Najm (left) and Asmar (right). Studio
Shehrazade, Saida, Lebanon,
1950s. Hashem el Madani
19.1 x 29

Anonymous. Studio Shehrazade,
Saida, Lebanon, early 1960s.
Hashem el Madani
19.1 x 24.5

Tate. Presented by Tate
International Council 2008

Hashem el Madani (1928–2017) was a prolific commercial photographer in Akram Zaatari's native Saida, Lebanon. In 1999, when Zaatari first visited Studio Shehrazade, he found Madani sitting on an archive of hundreds of thousands of negatives, recording the population of the coastal city throughout half a century. Exploring this material over subsequent years – a process he has compared to an archaeological dig – Zaatari produced a number of art projects, including films and repurposed selections of Madani's photography. The photographs shown here come from one such selection, printed and framed to Zaatari's specifications.

Zaatari spotted recurring themes within Madani's vast archive. In this compilation, we find small children, pairs of friends, and several clients posing with the same radio; like portrait photographers the world over, Madani kept a range of props to hand. After the 1967 war, long-haired Palestinians throng the studio, wearing flares and toting Kalashnikovs. In one shoot, a bodybuilder in sweaty trunks flexes astounding pectorals. But the main surprise may be these images, showing friends of the same sex kissing or playing at getting married. As the photographer explained it, the poses were a form of play-acting – in a conservative town where open displays of heterosexual romance would have been far more controversial. Their young sitters remain distant from our models of sexuality, but these vintage photographs have now been repackaged for us through Zaatari's capricious approach to excavation. This contemporary gay artist is inviting us to enjoy their acquired queerness.

Amid the theatrics, a singular face stands out. Ahmad el Abed was a gender-variant tailor in mid-century Saida, described by Madani as 'in-between man and woman'. With bouffant curls, perfectly groomed brows and modelling their own gender-neutral designs, Abed calmly holds our gaze across the distance of a lifetime.[61]

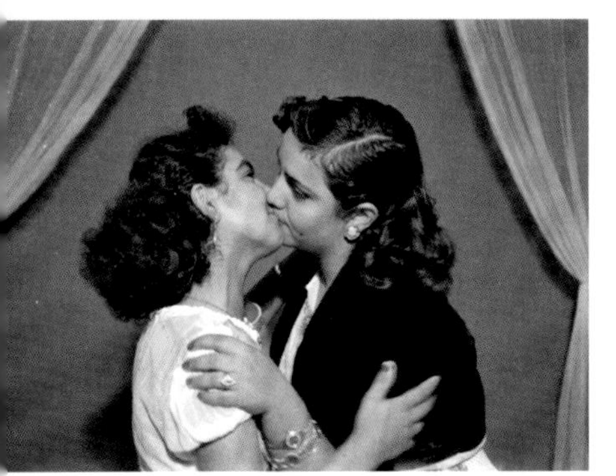
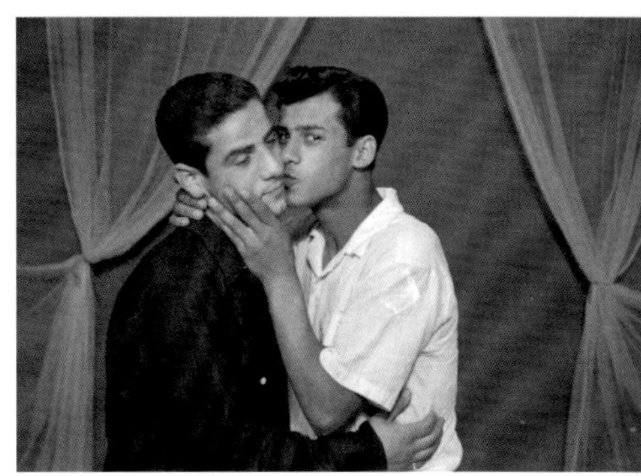
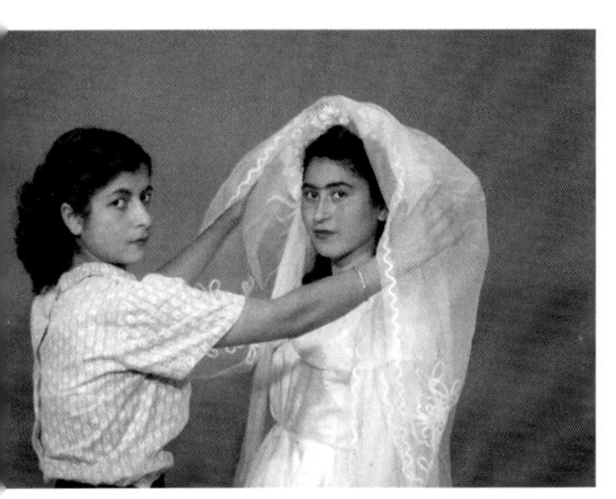
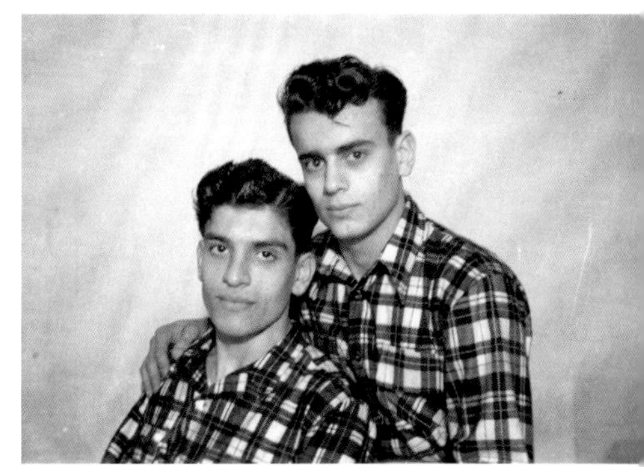
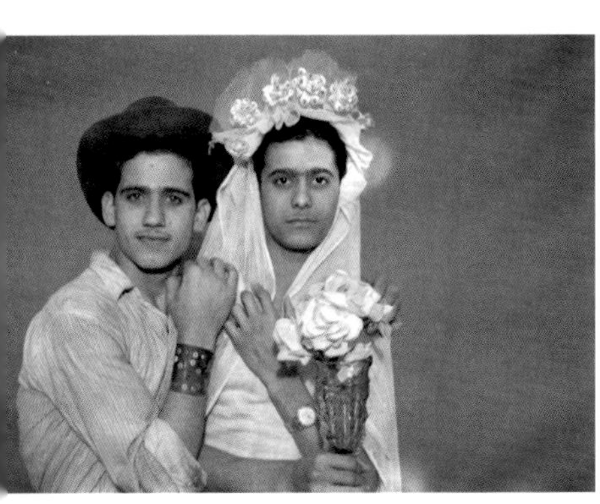
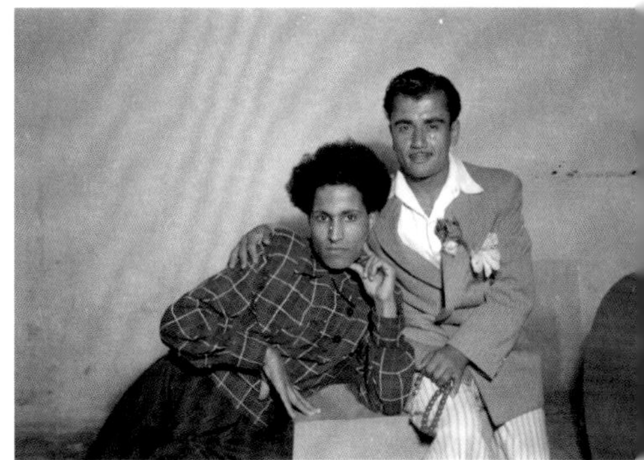

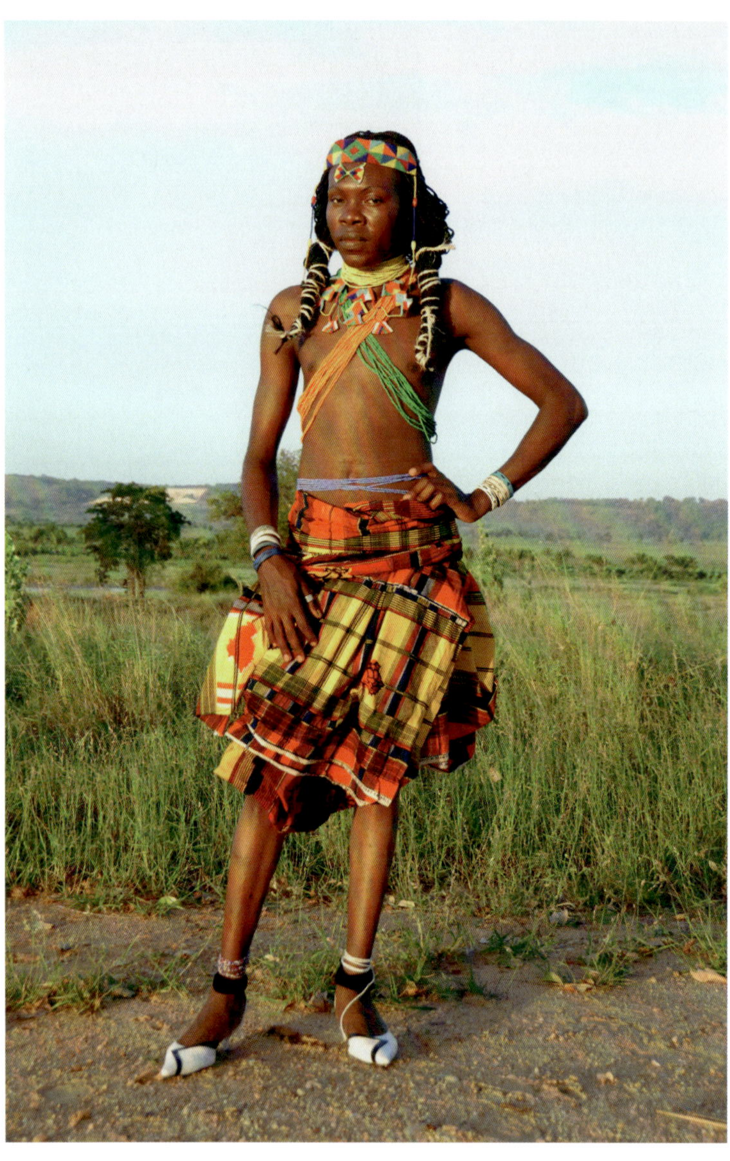

Kiluanji Kia Henda

b.1979 Angola
Poderosa de Bom Jesus

2008
Digital chromogenic print,
mounted on aluminium
165 x 110
Nuno De Lima Pimentel Collection

Poderosa de Bom Jesus appears to depict a figure in traditional tribal dress against a savanna backdrop. The image evokes a familiar documentary mode that so often purports to show us the real, authentic Africa. But Kiluanji Kia Henda is out to subvert such expectations.

Within an Angolan context, the style of outfit worn here is famously associated with women of the Mumuhuila people. These days, depressingly enough, foreign tourists are bussed to the country's rural south to snap their own ethnographic photographs of bare-breasted Mumuhuila women and girls. The picture opposite could almost be one such souvenir. Yet Bom Jesus is a municipality on the outskirts of Luanda, hundreds of miles to the north, and Poderosa's sex is male. Her luxuriant braids and plucked eyebrows point to a transgender town-dweller posing in tribal drag. 'Poderosa' means 'powerful one', but you hardly need Portuguese skills to clock 'Poderosa' as an awesome drag moniker. The kitten heels are the giveaway that there's precious little 'authenticity' to this performance. Mumuhuila women traditionally cake their hair with an earthy paste; Poderosa has simply wound her braids with twine. Her headdress looks fresh off a tourist souvenir stall.

Poderosa's half-hearted masquerade is slyly contrived. A ploy to wrong-foot 'the foreigner and his search for the exotic and "real" Africa', it satirises the white gaze and its fetish for bare skin and beads.[62] But Kia Henda also takes aim at a reductive notion of 'African tradition': an ideological mainstay of twenty-first-century homophobia, in Angola as elsewhere on the continent. Poderosa's queer restaging of tradition rattles the contemporary myth of an authentic, *straight* Africa.

Allyson Mitchell
b.1967 Canada
Ladies Sasquatch

2005–9
Textiles, wood, Styrofoam,
plastic, glass, fibreglass,
mechanical parts, lights,
found textiles
Overall dimensions variable
Private collection

Human imaginations have tended to paint Sasquatch (or Bigfoot) as a masculine, antisocial character: a sort of giant, unkempt hermit occasionally spied galumphing through remote habitats. Allyson Mitchell's vast installation of feminist Sasquatches offers a queer alternative. Among these six wild ladies, community and coiffure are core values.

Mitchell promotes her queer feminism via an impressive spread of activities. In addition to her exuberant visual art, she is a women's studies professor and, during the alternative, riot grrrl scene of the 1990s, was co-founder of a fat activist collective. With her partner, Deirdre Logue, Mitchell now runs a DIY Feminist Art Gallery (FAG for short) from their Toronto garage-studio.[63]

Advocating a maximalist art, Mitchell aims to use 'maximum materials, maximum emotion, maximum politics and maximum space'.[64] *Ladies Sasquatch* exemplifies the aesthetic. Her figures tower nine or ten feet tall (not counting pedestals). Their mighty physiques are a hotchpotch of repurposed materials: taxidermy prosthetics, unfashionable textiles, Halloween costumes and, most of all, fun fur – acres of it. As for the politics, Mitchell seizes the stereotype of the fat, hairy dyke, and shunts that to the maximum. The very terms used to dismiss or wound women have just been given legs – along with fangs and claws – and now return to fright the oppressor and lend snuggly protection to their sisters. Generously arrayed with nipples and prominent vulvas, the fat, furry embrace of Mitchell's ladies is surprisingly inviting. As the artist put it when the first two members of this community were exhibited, '*Lady Sasquatch* is your dream girl, only bigger and hairier – and she might eat you if you don't look out.'[65]

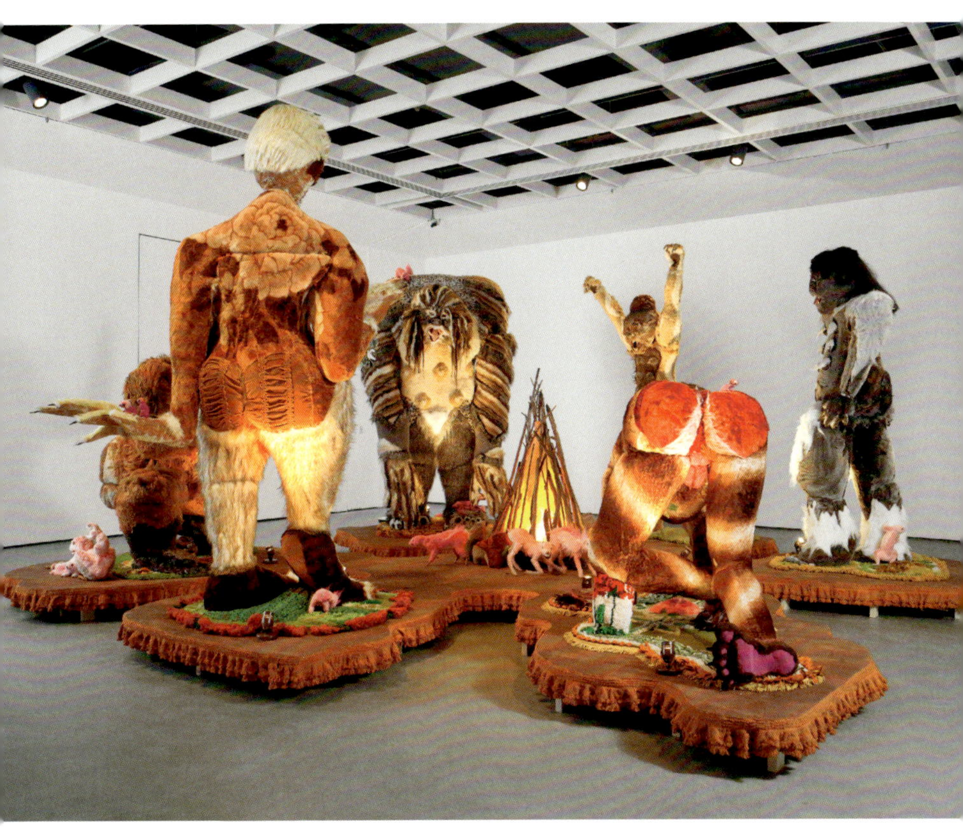

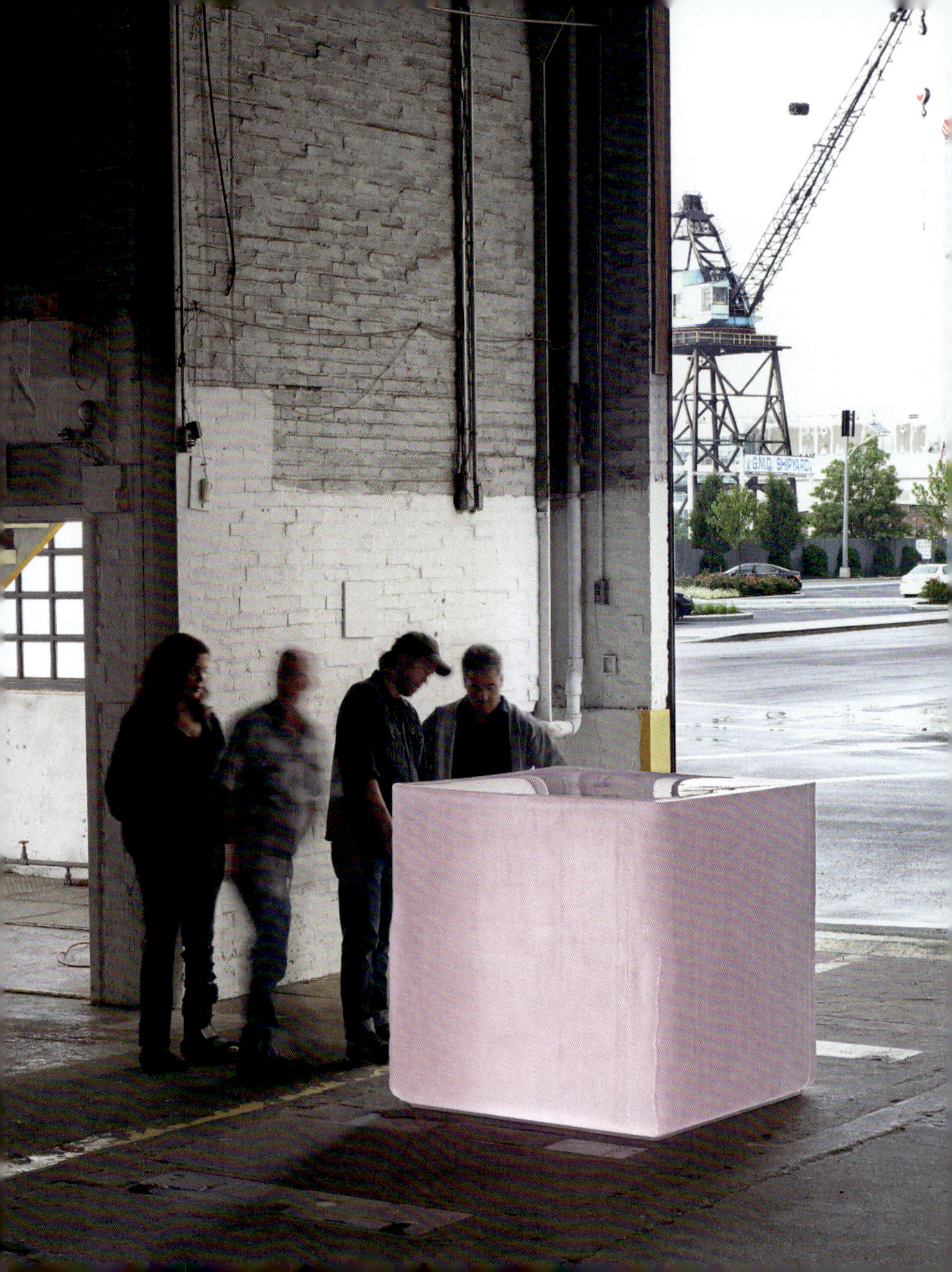

G.M.D. SHIPYARD

Roni Horn

b.1955 USA
Pink Tons

2008–11
Solid cast glass with as-cast
surfaces
121.9 x 121.9 x 121.9, 4,514 kg
Tate. Purchased with funds
provided by Tate Americas
Foundation, the North
American Acquisitions
Committee, the Art Fund,
Tate Members, Tate Patrons,
the artist and with additional
assistance from Dominque
Levy in honour of Dorothy
Berwin 2016

SPOILER ALERT: If this is your introduction to Roni Horn's *Pink Tons*, I urge you to put this book down. Go and take a look at Horn's sculpture for yourself. You'll find it positioned strategically, near one of Tate Modern's floor-to-ceiling windows. On a bright day, this solid cast block of glass becomes a mesmerising cube of roseate light. Photographs do it scant justice.

The habit of discerning gendered characteristics in abstract art comes out in force when *Pink Tons* is under scrutiny. Associations get touted that are hard to un-see. For a start, there's that 'pink' – few adjectives carry as much gendered baggage in Western culture. But here, that delicate shade is measured in hefty units. *Pink Tons* weighs as much as a medium-sized elephant; not every floor can safely support it. The scale and formal simplicity call to mind works by (male) American minimalist sculptors – the bare, metal boxes of Donald Judd (1928–94), for example. Yet Horn's artwork is not an exact cube, its flanks have subtle individualities, and there's not one sharp edge to be found. As you get close, the gleaming top slips away from the sides like the surface of liquid in a vessel. What should be solid masquerades as a vat of warm water – one you could happily slip inside.

Pink Tons is 'queer' in its strangeness; its physical properties cross categories, whether of modern art or everyday objects. But does a category-bending abstract sculpture have anything to say about gender? At the literal-minded extreme, one critic has hailed *Pink Tons* as 'a piece of transgender art', claiming it 'shouts "female" and "male" at the same time'.[66] I doubt that anyone would venture such readings without background knowledge of Roni Horn's much-commented-on androgyny. (And now you'll be stuck with those associations, like the rest of us.)

Lynette Yiadom-Boakye
b.1977 UK
The Generosity

2010
Oil paint on canvas
180 x 200
Tate. Presented by
Tate Patrons 2012

This could be the first painting in the history of art where all the action revolves around socks. Looking at *The Generosity*, it's difficult to decide whether the socks are coming off or going back on. But clearly, something has been afoot. Unless it's about to happen. One of the two men looks us right in the eye. Have we caught them in a transgressive act, prompting a hurried putting-on of socks? Or are you an invited spectator, waiting for them to begin? You won't find clues in the void that surrounds the pair.

Lynette Yiadom-Boakye peoples her artworks with an imagined cast of anonymous, but individualised, humans in indeterminate settings. Often a single figure just stands or sits there. They may either give us a look or ignore us, but don't expect them to unpack their secrets. Her two-handers and ensemble paintings have the same mute matter-of-factness: there they are, these people. Yiadom-Boakye also pens unsettling short stories, but she doesn't tell you the story in her paintings. If you want one, you need to provide your own. It's striking that her characters often provoke, but never enforce, a queer reading. Why are those two women holding hands? Why does this young man set my gaydar beeping? Yiadom-Boakye compels you to engage your imagination, but never gives you the easy satisfaction of a direct answer.

She may, however, let slip a clue. In a conversation with Glenn Ligon (pp.104–5), Yiadom-Boakye has described *The Generosity* as 'one of the most romantic things I've ever done'. With a chuckle, she adds: 'it just says it all – about what we *all* want … the kind of love we're all looking for.'[67]

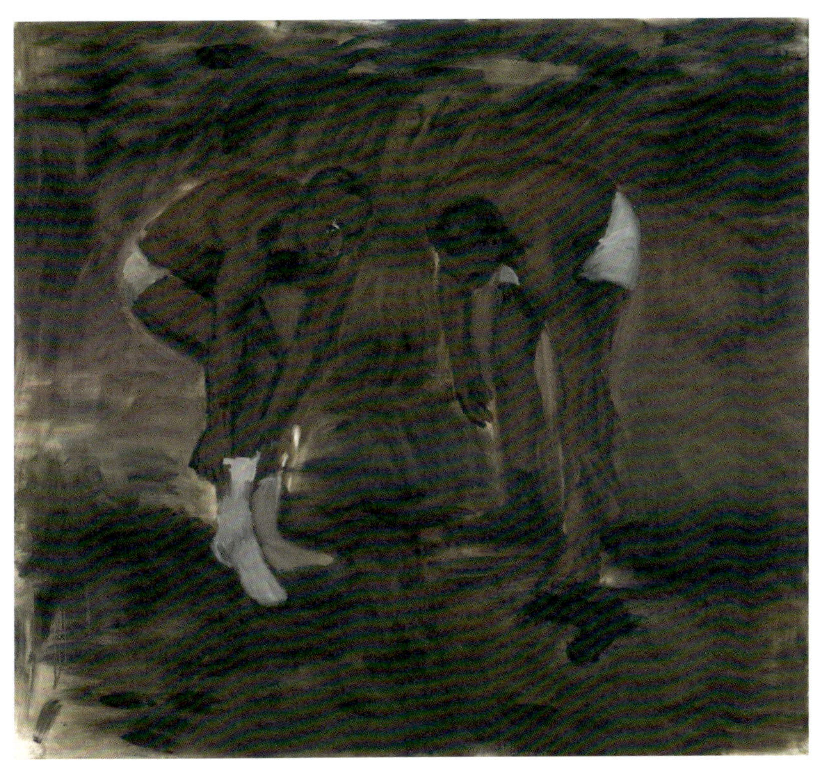

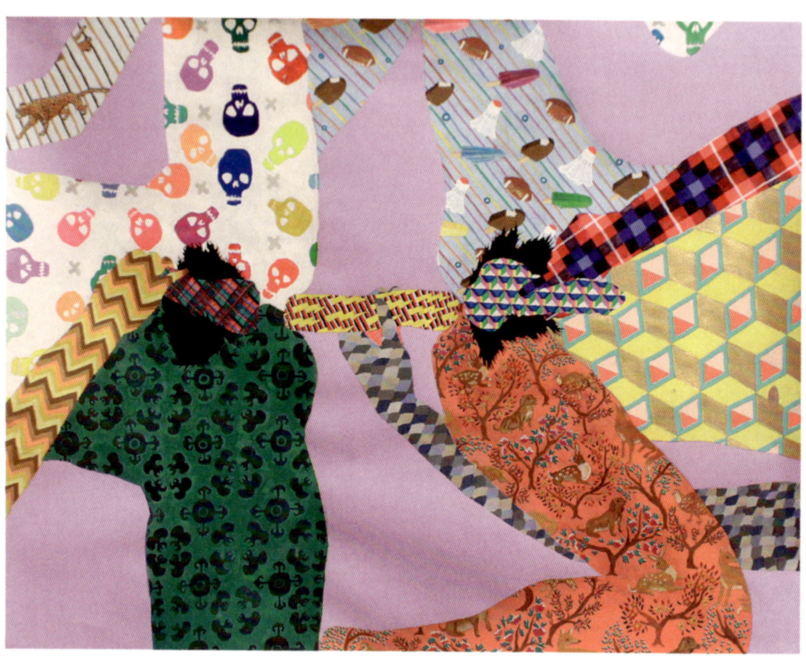

Mark Aguhar
1987–2012 USA
No Top Needed

2010
Graphite, ink, gouache
and watercolour on paper
50 x 64.5
Private collection

It can take a moment to discern what we are looking at amid Mark Aguhar's riot of lovingly painted patterns. *No Top Needed* shows two naked figures from above, cut off at the midriff. In a literal sense, the tops of these bodies aren't required for the image to work. And yet, hairstyles, faces and chests – along with clothes – supply our habitual reference points for guessing at gender identities. Here, such anchors have been removed, just as indicators of race are withheld by patterning the parts we can see. Controlling the parameters of the image, the artist frustrates our routine assessments of social positioning. In this context, of course, 'top' refers to a dominant or penetrating partner during sex. These two queer bottoms, linked by a double-ended dildo, are doing fine by themselves. *No Top Needed* extols cooperative self-reliance. In this blissful, queer equilibrium, neither bottom has to 'switch' (take on the top role) to fill an absence.

The emancipatory message delivered in flippant packaging was often Aguhar's chosen tactic. Among the artist's most quoted statements is her pseudo-offhand remark: 'I love being flippant, flippancy is the most important thing in the world.'[68] Aguhar used her drawings, performances, pithy inscriptions and blog posts to voice dissent from structures of social power that marginalised her as 'a genderqueer person of color fat femme fag feminist'.[69] The results, as *No Top Needed* demonstrates, use provocative wit to deflate the mystique of all varieties of dominance. This is an image that puts the 'subversive' into 'sub/dom', suggesting our identities can find fulfilment outside of the relentless pursuit of our supposed complements.

Edie Fake
b.1980 USA
Club LaRay

2012
From *Memory Palaces*
Ballpoint pen, ink and gouache
on paper
61 x 48 (approx.)
Private collection

The traces of queer lives in the past seep through chinks in the historical record like pungent vapours. Inhale these fumes and half-glimpsed visions fill your head. *Did they really do that? What really went on in that party? that bathhouse? … that bedroom?* It's fitting that so much queer writing – from Christopher Marlowe's *Edward II* to the novels of Sarah Waters – resurrects the ghosts of queer ancestors. We somehow need to affirm that *such people were*, before we were, and that no regime that punishes deviance has ever eliminated the defiant expression of difference.

It is on this smoking soil that Edie Fake's *Memory Palaces* are built. From advertisements in vintage magazines, the artist harvested former sites of queer pleasure or feminist activism in his native Chicago. Names from the 1970s, like The Snake Pit (a gay bar) or *Killer Dyke* (a student newspaper) have long gone from the city's streets, if they ever had a visible address. Fake has recreated them all as imaginary architectural wonders. Club LaRay (opened 1986, forcibly closed 1989) was a mainly black, gay venue, attracting crowds of young dancers for nightly helpings of local house music and legendary drag acts. In Fake's version, the whole façade of *Club LaRay* seems to pulsate to the music within.

Gorgeously ornamental, but structurally dodgy, these are palaces of the mind and determinedly neither acts of mourning nor preservation. The artist has described them as a 'resource for the present'.[70] Each oversized door invites us to enter and partake in an ongoing collective project: to realise dreams of liberated, queer forms of living.

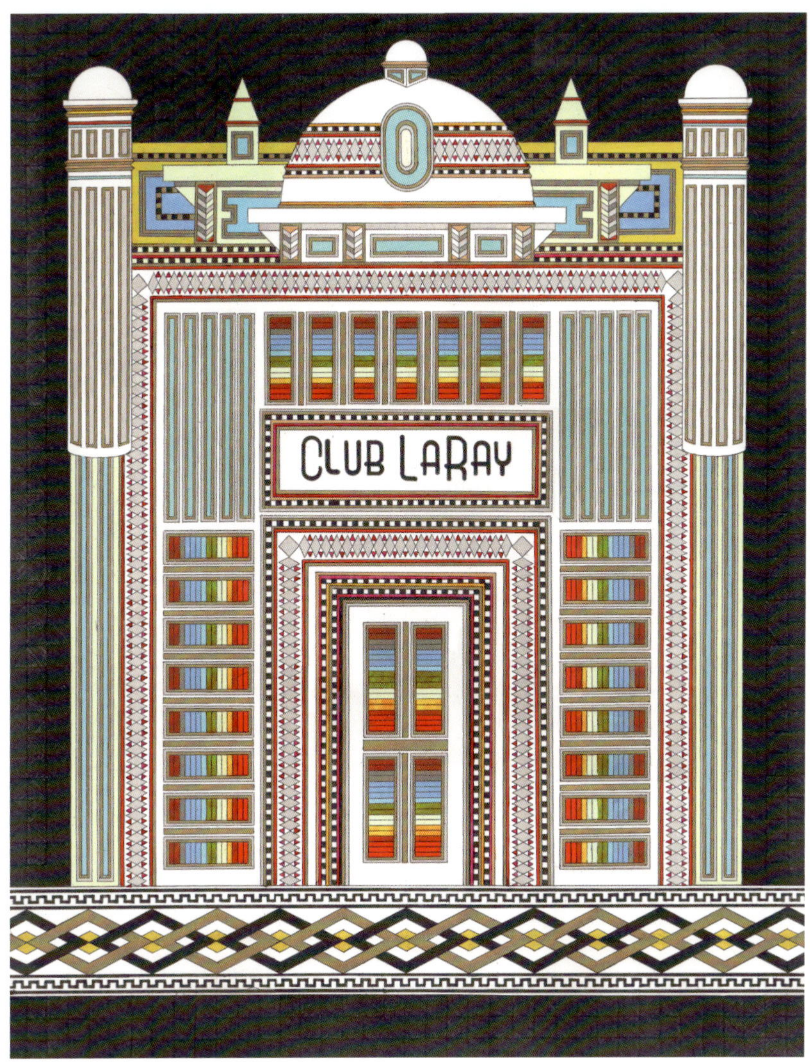

CLUB LaRay

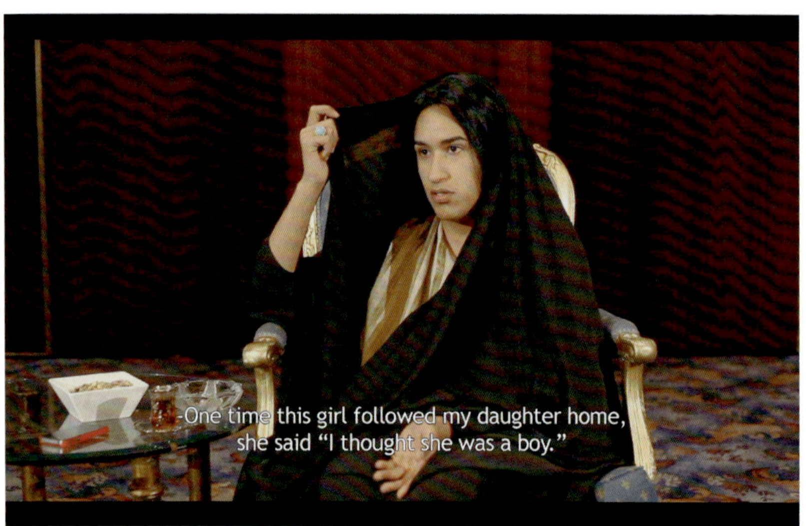
-One time this girl followed my daughter home,
she said "I thought she was a boy."

Fatima Al Qadiri
b.1981 Senegal,
lives Germany
Khalid al Gharaballi
b.1981 Kuwait
*Mendeel Um A7mad
(NxIxSxM)*

2012
Giant replica tissue box, screening
room inside, HD video loop
Video duration: 15 min, 28 sec

With *Mendeel Um A7mad (NxIxSxM)*, Fatima Al Qadiri and Khalid al Gharaballi gently satirise the mores of Kuwaiti society. Their video stages a female social ritual of late-morning hospitality and tea drinking. It uses a critical device common in queer film and performance: mimicking the normative realm to render it strange.

The opulence of wealthy Kuwaiti homes is comically amplified by filming in a grand hotel reception hall. The self-satisfied hostess, Majida, and her guests, Nadia, Iqbal and Sarah, conduct their dialogue from chairs spaced absurdly far apart. Barbed remarks begin to fly at long range as soon as the drinks trolley (wheeled by a silent Filipino housemaid) has completed its tortuously slow circuit.

All four women are played by men and, though the actors bring acute observation to their performances, the casting places the dialogue in queer inverted commas. The effect reaches its ironic peak as the women lament the visible queer presence in public space. As Sarah complains: 'You don't know who's male or female in the country anymore!' They talk with alarm of *boyat*: masculine-presenting young women. 'They're everywhere,' Nadia grumbles, '... girls holding hands with their butch girlfriends.' With the cast struggling not to smile at points, these straight anxieties around gender rule-breaking lose their normative foothold.

Mendeel Um A7mad (NxIxSxM) is that rarest of finds: a work of contemporary art that's genuinely funny. Yet the video's end credits are sobering; only one actor's name is given. Gender transgression, playful or earnest, is risky in present-day Kuwait. Five years before this installation was first shown in the capital, Kuwait's parliament criminalised any act of 'imitating the opposite sex'. Police harassment of the Gulf state's trans population surged after the law change. Prosecutions, fines and imprisonment have become a real threat.

Tomoko Kashiki
b.1982 Japan
Forget Me (Not)

2013
Acrylic paint on linen,
mounted on wooden panel
227 x 145
Private collection

Describing her painstaking process of making paintings, Tomoko Kashiki speaks of one driving ambition: 'to realise beauty'.[71] Such single-mindedness pays off. The works of this artist are consistently delightful to the senses, even when they unsettle us with their imagery. Though Kashiki favours the modern medium of acrylic paints, her laboriously layered colours evoke much older Japanese painting practices using natural mineral pigments. The legacy of 'traditional' or *nihonga* art can also be felt in Kashiki's calligraphic outlines and her avoidance of shadows.

These exquisite pictures enchant viewers into a unique imaginative world. Its slender, androgynous inhabitants display a ghostlike fluidity of form, in tune with the woozy perspective Kashiki often uses to structure the surrounding space: walls and limbs similarly malleable. Norms of the physical world are set aside. Floods sweep through interiors without explanation. 'Solid' ground moves in rippling waves. Gravity loosens its grip on attenuated bodies swayed by the softest of breezes.

Kashiki's characters are often solitary, but in *Forget Me (Not)* they seem to be enjoying each other's company as they bob, naked, in a bubbling pool. Things are, literally, getting steamy: clouds obscuring upper reaches of the cavernous space. Yet Kashiki's eroticism is delicately expressed. Towards the left edge, one pair, fingers lightly entwined, spread long limbs to nestle half-submerged bodies. In their free hands, each figure grips a stem of the eponymous blue flower, which in Japan – as in Europe – traditionally signifies true love. Their gangly frames are non-specific as to gender. And, though it may be tempting to read significance into their painted nails, the artist has stressed she did not intend to categorise her bathers as either female or male.

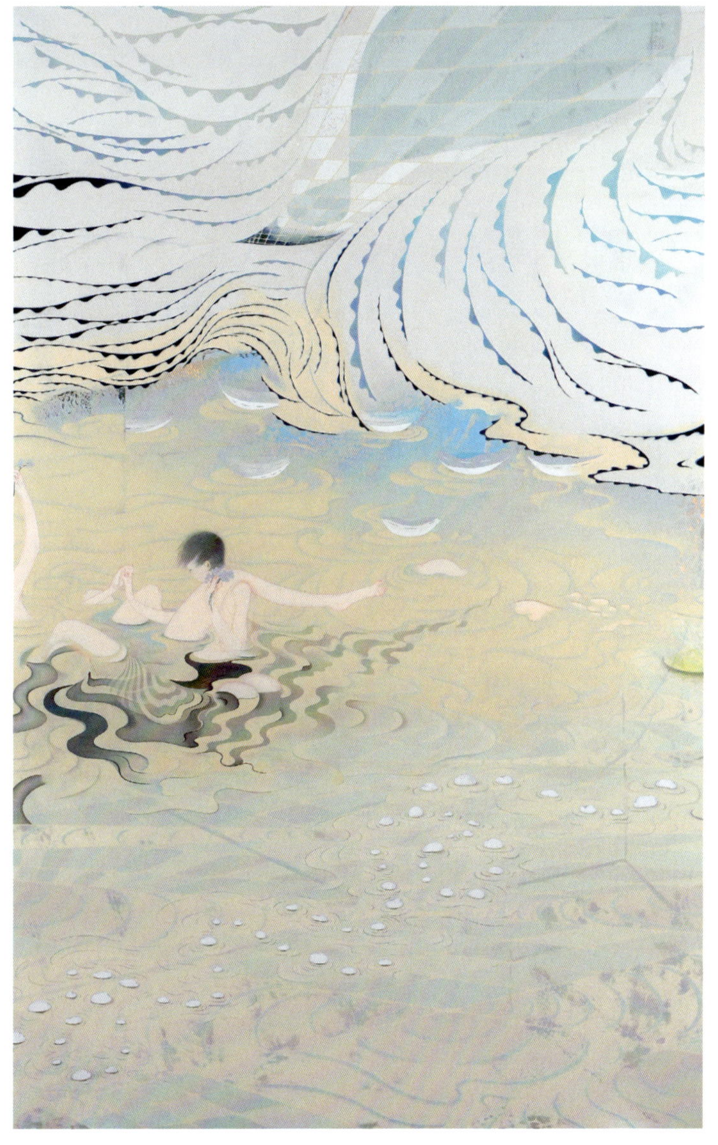

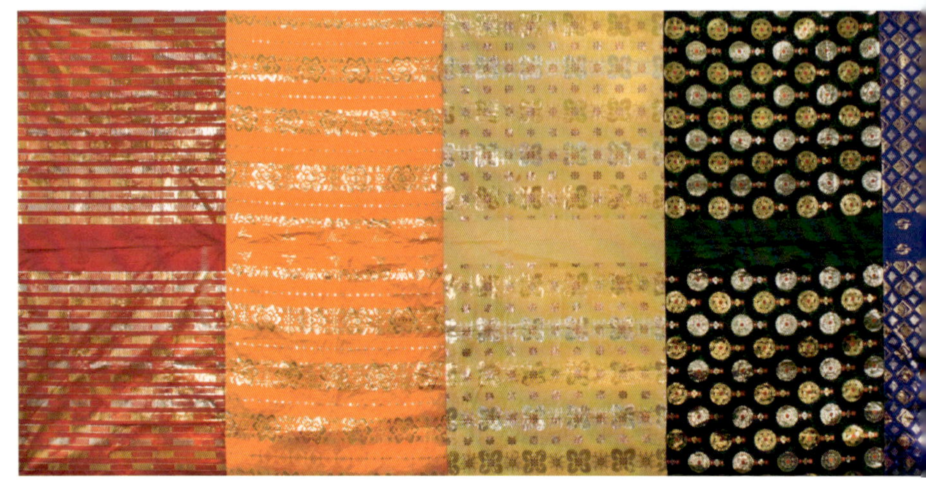

Adejoke Tugbiyele

b.1977 USA

Gele Pride Flag

2014
Mechanically woven jacquard
fabric with metallic thread
130 x 400 (approx.)
Collection of the artist

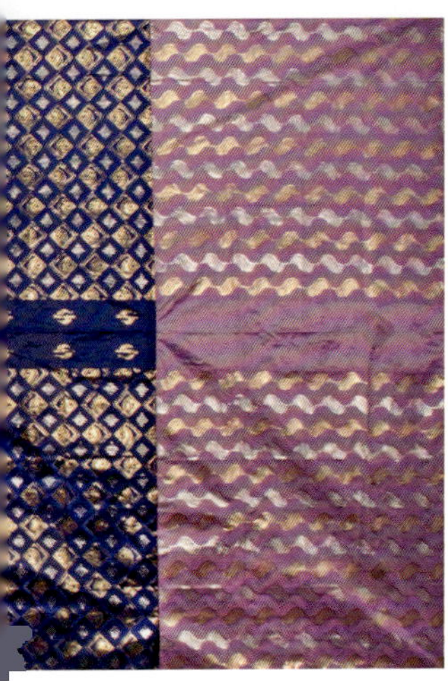

In her mid-30s, Adejoke Tugbiyele took a graduate class on the work of Rotimi Fani-Kayode (pp.98–9). She has described the precedent of this earlier queer Yoruba artist as 'the ultimate ass-kick I needed to move forward with ideas of my sexual identity in my work'.[72] In sculptures, drawings and performances created since that turning point, the artist frequently explores queer experience or tackles homophobia head on.

Tugbiyele happened to be on a working visit to Nigeria, where she was part-raised, around the time that the Same-Sex Marriage (Prohibition) Act, 2013 was signed into law. The artist agreed to talk on air about this aggressively anti-gay legislation, becoming one of the first queer women in Nigeria to speak so publicly about her sexuality. Before she left the country, the artist made *Gele Pride Flag*.

Colourful and expansive, *gele* head wraps are a distinctive feature of Yoruba women's style. Tugbiyele may not, herself, wear this feminine accessory, but has 'always admired it for its aesthetic properties'. Stung by the vocal homophobia surrounding the law change, Tugbiyele bought six *gele* cloths and stitched them into this rainbow flag: an international symbol for LGBT pride. It was a gesture that, she says, 'helped me affirm my queerness as a woman of Nigerian heritage'.[73] *Gele Pride Flag* has been taken out on Pride parades and to a protest against Nigeria's anti-gay law at the country's New York embassy. This CV lends it an unusual status: part artwork, part protest banner. Fitting, for an artist who argues 'political art … must engage people and serve as a call to action'.[74]

Athi-Patra Ruga
b.1984 South Africa
*Proposed Model of
the New Azanian*

2014
Wool, thread and artificial
flowers on tapestry canvas
444.5 x 162.6
Elizabeth A. Sackler Center for
Feminist Art, Brooklyn Museum,
New York

Welcome to Azania. The name has belonged both to a region in Africa's remote past and to an ideal, post-colonial nation: an unachieved dream that sustained decades of anti-apartheid struggle. Athi-Patra Ruga's Azania inherits aspects of these namesakes, but its territory, inhabitants and legends issue forth – in glorious Technicolor – from the imagination of this young South African artist. With good reason, Ruga displays a queer scepticism towards rigid national identities. His childhood was lived between the Bantustans of apartheid's dying decade; every day meant crossing 'international' borders unrecognised beyond South Africa. In those same, pain-filled years, vanguard organisations resorted to killing in the name of Azanian liberation. Ruga's reinvention of Azania can be seen almost as a project of healing.

The project kicked off in 2010 with the debut of *The Future White Woman of Azania*: Ruga's drag performance avatar for the next six years. The Future White Woman was both hidden and impossible to miss – her face and body concealed inside a colourful cloud of latex balloons. Her compatriots have emerged via a gaudy series of tapestries and sculptures. These are flavour-enhanced artworks that flout old-school distinctions; fine art versus craft, avant-garde versus kitsch – such polarities collapse in Ruga's Azanian portrait gallery.

Norms are also disregarded when it comes to imagining the citizenry. The *Proposed Model of the New Azanian* is an uncanny fusion of male and female. Cultural and ethnic markers are likewise blurred. The flickering colours of tapestry wool might stand for most known skin colours or perhaps all, simultaneously. The headdress combines Greco-Roman laurel wreath with Arab-style *keffiyeh*. This giant ambassador represents a homeland for all, the preserve of none.

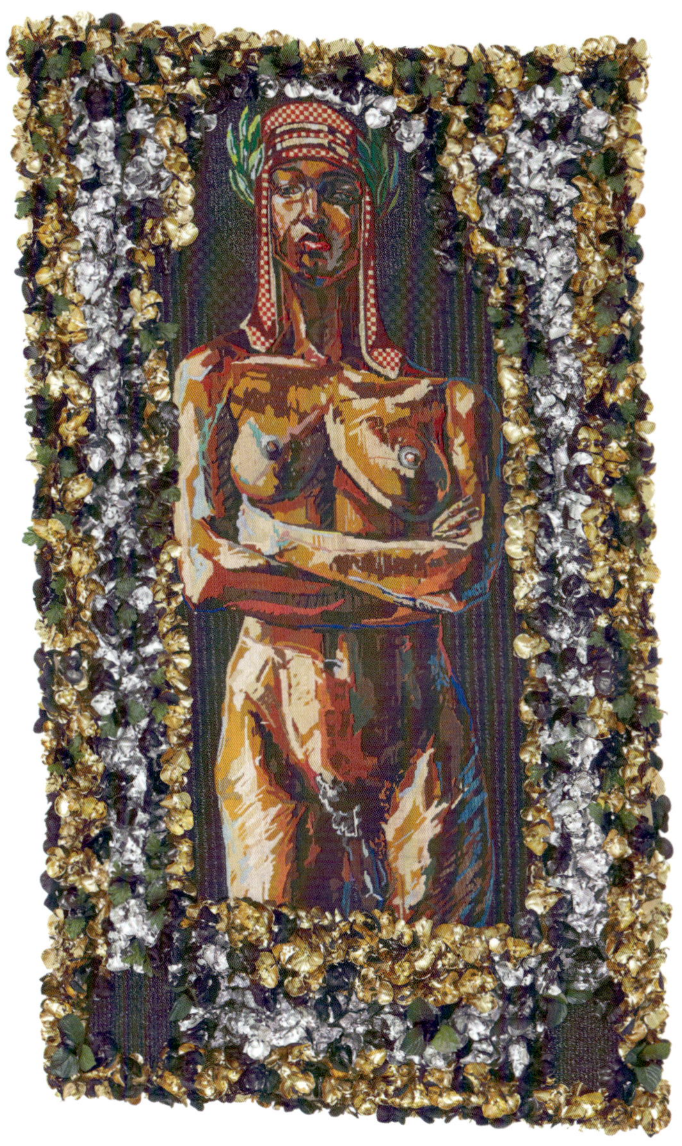

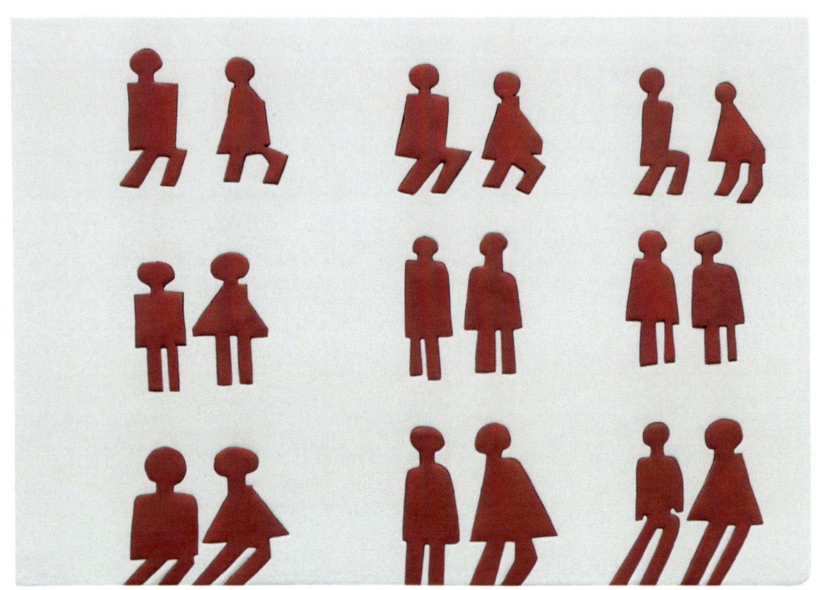

Sadie Benning

b.1973 USA

Bathroom People

2014
Medite, aqua resin,
casein and enamel
95.3 x 137.2
Private collection

What's your sign? Does it have a triangular or a rectangular body?

Within public space, we encounter enclaves that only around half the population are eligible to enter. Shop fitting rooms, changing facilities, toilets – they all come in twos, and only one is meant for you. But what if neither is? What if your body is neither a triangle nor a rectangle, or if others regularly think it's one when it's actually the other?

For those such as artist Sadie Benning, who live as a non-binary gender, or for anyone whose gender is ever questioned, crossing sex-specific thresholds is a daily cause of mild anxiety at best. In some environments, those perceived as being in the 'wrong' space risk public humiliation or much worse. The issue of equal access to such spaces for transgender, intersex or gender nonconforming people was already starting to rumble in the US when Benning made this painting in 2014. At the time of writing, two years later, it has become the most aggressive front in America's culture wars. State legislatures have now debated dozens of 'bathroom bills' that seek to make access to these facilities dependent on having a matching birth certificate: a stipulation that directly discriminates against most transgender people.

In Benning's *Bathroom People*, the conventional signage for the two most widely-recognised genders is put through a queer mangle. Can you always recognise the triangles and rectangles? What changes when both sit down? And what if that 'gender trouble', perceived today as a marginal, transgender experience, were to become something shared by all?

Notes

1 From Stiller's perspective, very local indeed: Carl Milles lived little more than a mile from the AB Svenska Biografteatern studio on the island of Lidingö, where the film *The Wings* was produced.

2 2 Jun.–12 Aug. 2007, Migros Museum für Gegenwartskunst, Zurich. The exhibition was later translated into the form of an artist's book: Henrik Olesen, *Some Faggy Gestures*, Zurich 2008.

3 *UBS Openings: Saturday Live Mumbai*, 16 Sept. 2007, Tate Modern. *Encounter(s)* was also performed that year at The Tramway, Glasgow and Fondazione Sandretto Re Rebaudengo, Turin.

4 Matt Houlbrook, *Queer London: Perils and Pleasures in the Sexual Metropolis, 1918–1957*, Chicago and London 2005, p.55.

5 The figure clambering into the boat is lifted from a group of bathing soldiers in Michelangelo's mural composition, *The Battle of Cascina* 1504–6, known only through sixteenth-century copies.

6 Quoted in Richard Shone, *Bloomsbury Portraits*, London 1993, p.64.

7 Jean Rook, 'Waiting for Bowie, and finding a genius who insists he's really a clown', *Daily Express*, 5 May 1976. http://www.bowiegoldenyears.com/articles/760505-dailyexpress.html.

8 Robert Montenegro, *Vaslav Nijinsky: An Artistic Interpretation of his Work in Black, White and Gold*, London 1913.

9 Robert Ross (ed.), Oscar Wilde, *De Profundis*, 2nd edn, New York 1909, p.106.

10 Oscar Wilde, *The Sphinx*, with decorations by Charles Ricketts, London 1894. Vaslav Nijinsky choreographed and starred in the Ballets Russes production, *L'Après-midi d'un faune* (premiered in May 1912). Examples of hybrid bodies in contemporary art include works by Chitra Ganesh, Nandipha Mntambo and Wangechi Mutu.

11 The elfin figure, far left, who rests his hand on the centaur's shoulder adopts a pose found in several works by Signorelli: *The Court of Pan* c.1484 (destroyed 1945); *Figures in a Landscape: Man, Woman and Child* c.1440 (Toledo Museum of Art, Toledo OH); *The Resurrection of the Flesh* 1500–4 (San Brizio Chapel, Orvieto Cathedral). Only the Orvieto example includes the head-turn over the shoulder (and also belongs in a love triangle).

12 Transcript of a taped interview (1975), in George Plimpton, *Truman Capote: In which Various Friends, Enemies, Acquaintances, and Detractors Recall his Turbulent Career*, New York 1998, p.86. Capote's studio visit took place in 1948.

13 Claude Cahun, *Aveux non avenus*, Paris 1930, as *Disavowals*, trans. Susan de Muth, London 2007, p.151.

14 Hannah Höch, 'Catalogue foreword to Hannah Höch's first solo exhibition at the Kunstzaal De Bron, The Hague; Rotterdamsche Kring, Rotterdam; Kunstzaal Van Lier, Amsterdam, 1929', in *Hannah Höch*, exh. cat., Whitechapel Gallery, London 2014, p.140.

15 This argument is made powerfully by Michelle Doré Sizemore in 'Undefined & indefinable: Androgynous imagery in the work of Hannah Höch', MA thesis, University of Connecticut 2013, pp.47–53.

16 Toyen, *Untitled* 1932, private collection; reproduced in *Toyen*, exh. cat., City Gallery Prague 2000, p.97, pl.108.

17 Frida Kahlo, *The Two Fridas* 1939, Museo de Arte Moderno, Mexico City.

18 Margaret Rose Vendryes, *Barthé: A Life in Sculpture*, Jackson, MS 2008, pp.120–8.

19 'Homintern' was a pun on the Communist International – or 'Comintern' for short. The idea that an international clique of gay men wielded supreme influence in the arts was a popular mid-century conspiracy theory.

20 Arcadia is a rural province of southern Greece, associated since antiquity with an idyllic, pastoral way of life. Craxton's queer Arcadia is even more obvious in *Shepherds near Knossos* 1947: a related painting in which one of the two young men languorously reclines on a hillside.

21 The artist was speaking with reference to his earlier works on English pastoral themes. Interview with Gerard Hastings, published in *John Craxton: An Exhibition of Paintings and Drawings 1980–1985*, exh. cat., Christopher Hull Gallery, London 1985, pp.21–3.

22 Andy Warhol, interviewed in Gene R. Swenson, 'What is pop art? Answers from eight painters, part 1', *Art News*, vol.62, no.7, Nov. 1963, p.26.

23 *Studies for a Boy Book* by Andy Warhol, 14 Feb. – 3 Mar. 1956, Bodley Gallery and Bookshop, New York. (The promised book didn't materialize.)

24 The original ballpoint drawing for *Male Nude* appeared in a recent online auction. *Andy Warhol @ Christie's: For Members Only: Eyes on the Guise*, 13–27 Jun. 2013, lot 144. https://onlineonly.christies. com/s/andy-warhol-christies- members-only-eyes-guise/male- nude-144/727

25 *The Origin of the World* (Musée d'Orsay, Paris) is Courbet's close- up of a naked woman, legs spread wide, from upper abdomen to mid- thigh. Aside from the hands (not shown by Courbet), Warhol's *Male Nude* almost mirrors the painting's composition.

26 The quote is from Ted Carey, in Patrick S. Smith, *Warhol: Conversations about the Artist*, Ann Arbor and London 1988, p.94.

27 Eikoh Hosoe, *Bara-kei*, Tokyo 1963. The initial English version of the book's title was 'Killed by Roses'. It was Mishima who insisted on the adjusted translation in 1970, in the run-up to a new edition of *Bara-kei*. Eikoh Hosoe, 'Subject Matter', transcript of a talk, published 1 Jun. 2010 on *American Suburb X*. http://www.americansuburbx. com/2010/06/eikoh-hosoe- subject-matter.html

28 Yukio Mishima, introduction, *Yukio Mishima Exhibition*, exh. cat., Tobu department store, Tokyo 1970; quoted in Henry Scott Stokes, *The Life and Death of Yukio Mishima*, revised edn, New York 1995, p.181.

29 The painting is, in part, a replica of Giorgione's *Sleeping Venus* (c.1510, Gemäldegalerie Alte Meister, Dresden).

30 Robert Indiana, 'Artist questionnaire', 11 Dec. 1961, Object Files, Department of Painting and Sculpture, Museum of Modern Art, New York. Printed in *Robert Indiana: Beyond Love*, exh. cat., Whitney Museum of American Art, New York 2013, p.205.

31 Indiana's Coenties Slip neighbours included Agnes Martin and Lenore Tawney, then in a relationship, and Indiana's own lover Ellsworth Kelly. Cy Twombly lived nearby and employed Indiana's spacious studio. Robert Rauschenberg and Jasper Johns were a few streets away and known

to Indiana through mutual friends Kelly and Twombly.

32 More specifically, Indiana's beams have haunched tenons. The corresponding mortise forms the 'female' side of the joint.

33 Quoted in Christopher Reed, *Art and Homosexuality: A History of Ideas*, Oxford and New York 2011, p.171. Hockney's fascination with a California he had yet to visit is an update on the sunny, Mediterranean queer idylls often romanticised by earlier British artists, including Ethel Walker, Glyn Philpot and John Craxton.

34 Nikos Stangos (ed.), *David Hockney by David Hockney*, London 1976, p.99 (for the quotation). Paul Melia, 'Showers, pools and power', in Paul Melia (ed.), *David Hockney*, Manchester 1995, pp.56–7 (on the voyeuristic angle).

35 In the top row: José Martí (far left), Camilo Cienfuegos and Juan Almeida Bosque (to the right of Lenin and Ho Chi Minh). Che Guevara features in close-up at the start of the second row. Fidel Castro addresses a battery of microphones on the right-hand side.

36 David Sylvester, *The Brutality of Fact: Interviews with Francis Bacon*, 3rd edn, London 1988, p.76.

37 Michael Peppiatt, *Francis Bacon in the 1950s*, Norwich 2006, p.31.

38 TateShots: Barkley L. Hendricks – 'I Want to Be Memorable', video podcast, 28 Jul. 2016 https://www.youtube.com/ watch?v=VIRHKivQCqw

39 Ibid.

40 Besides his four portraits of Taylor, Hendricks painted a bold image of an interracial gay couple: *Hasty Tasty* 1977 (The Museum of Fine Arts, Houston).

41 Carla Macchiavello, 'Marking the territory: Performance, video, and conceptual graphics in Chilean art, 1975–1985', PhD thesis, Stony Brook University 2010, p.71. The contest was hosted by Galería Módulos y Formas, Santiago.

42 *Black Woman Time Now*, 30 Nov.–31 Dec. 1983, Battersea Arts Centre, London.

43 In works such as *Freedom and Change* (1984), *Between the Two my Heart is Balanced* and *Ankledeep* (both 1991, Tate).

44 Hockney painted a number of large-scale double portraits of gay friends: *Christopher Isherwood and Don Bachardy* (1968, private collection); *Henry Geldzahler and Christopher Scott* (1969, private collection); *George Lawson and Wayne Sleep* (1972–5, Tate).

45 Respectively: *Packing*; *Crying*; *Taking Drugs*; *Trying to Sleep*; and *God, I Miss Him So Much.*

46 Robb Hernández, *VIVA Records, 1970–2000: Lesbian and Gay Latino Artists of Los Angeles*, The Chicano Archives, vol.7, Los Angeles 2013, pp.27–8.

47 For examples (and the background to St Sebastian's queer history), see Richard A. Kaye, 'Losing his religion: Saint Sebastian as contemporary gay martyr', in Peter Horne and Reina Lewis (eds.), *Outlooks: Lesbian and Gay Sexualities and Visual Cultures*, London and New York 1996, pp.86–105; and *Saint Sebastian: A Splendid Readiness for Death*, exh. cat., Kunsthalle Wien, Vienna 2003.

48 A selection of these comments, gathered from six tour locations, appears in the accompanying postcard book: Kiss & Tell, *Drawing the Line: Lesbian Sexual Politics on the Wall*, Vancouver 1991.

49 Linda Simpson, 'A memorial for drag icon Miss Demeanor', *Art F City*, 23 Jun. 2014. http://artfcity.com/2014/06/23/a-memorial-for-drag-icon-miss-demeanor/

50 *Wolfgang Tillmans: if one thing matters, everything matters*, exhibition, Tate Britain 6 Jun. – 5 Sept. 2003.

51 Respectively: *Faltenwurf (oliv)* (1996), *chaos cup* (1997) and *Kate sitting* (1996) – all Tate collection.

52 'Peter Halley in conversation with Wolfgang Tillmans', in Jan Verwoert, Peter Halley, Wolfgang Tillmans and Midori Matsui, *Wolfgang Tillmans*, Phaidon Contemporary Artists, London 2002, pp.26–8.

53 Respectively: *moonrise, Puerto Rico* (1995), *Faltenwurf (oliv)* (1996) and *Stilleben Marktstrasse* (1997) – all Tate collection.

54 When *ID Crisis* featured in Muholi's first solo exhibition (2004), a caption from the artist encouraged a narrower reading of this figure as a troubled young lesbian who feels compelled to 'pass' due to a lack of available lesbian role models. See Henriette Gunkel, 'Through the postcolonial eyes: Images of gender and female sexuality in contemporary South Africa', in Sara E. Cooper (ed.), *Lesbian Images in International Popular Culture*, special issue of the *Journal of Lesbian Studies*, Abingdon and New York 2010, pp.74–6.

55 Prints of *Aftermath* (2004) and *Ordeal*, *Bra* and *In-security* (all 2003) are also in the Tate collection.

56 I suspect this usage goes back to the 1970s. It was familiar enough by the early 1980s to be chosen as the slogan of 1982's Boston Pride.

57 Karol Radziszewski: *Pedały* ('Fags'), private apartment, 20 Włościańska Street, Warsaw, 21 Jun. – 5 Jul. 2005.

58 Karol Radziszewski, 'In search for queer ancestors', trans. by Ewa Kowal, L'Internationale, 15 Feb. 2016. http://www.internationaleonline.org/research/decolonising_practices/55_in_search_for_queer_ancestors

59 Hanna Rydlewska, Barbara Welbel, 'Jestem pedałem, jeszcze o wystawie Karola Radziszewskiego', Obieg, 28 May 2005. http://archiwum-obieg.u-jazdowski.pl/893
Precedents in Poland for artist-operated galleries run from private apartments include Ewa Partum's Address Gallery in Łódź and Warsaw's Studio of Activities, Documentation and Propagation, run by KwieKulik (Zofia Kulik and

Przemysław Kwiek); both were active in the 1970s.

60 Ganesh draws principally on a vast library of stories that Indian comics house Amar Chitra Katha has published since the late 1960s. Like many children of the South Asian diaspora growing up in the 1970s and 80s, Ganesh absorbed these English-language comic retellings of history, myth and ancient epics alongside Western comics.

61 The quotation from Madani comes from the subtitles of Akram Zaatari's film, *Twenty-Eight Nights and a Poem* (Lebanon/France 2015). The photographer goes on to say that Abed 'regarded himself in the same category as women – psychologically'. Zaatari added the detail about Abed's self-designed clothes during a Q&A session after a screening of the film at Tate Modern, 11 May 2016.

62 Kia Henda, quoted in Garreth van Niekerk, 'To be young, gifted and black', *City Press Trending*, 4 Oct. 2015. http://city-press. news24.com/Trending/To-be-young-gifted-and-black-20151005
To Kia Henda's dismay, some viewers at the São Paulo Biennial found Poderosa's tribal realness all too convincing. Rachel Nelson, 'Kiluanji Kia Henda: Art beyond the local and the global', *SAVVY: Journal of Contemporary African Art*, Bonaventure Soh Bejeng Ndikung and Andrea Heister (eds.), Fall 2012, pp.84–5. See also: Nadine Siegert, 'The archive as construction site: Collective memory and trauma in contemporary art from Angola',

World Art, vol.6, no.1, 2016, pp.116–8.

63 https://www.facebook.com/ FeministArtGallery

64 Allyson Mitchell quoted in Jeremy Hof, 'Lady Maximus: Allyson Mitchell', *Border Crossings*, vol.28, no.3, Aug. 2009, p.21.

65 Artist's statement on exhibition web page: *Allyson Mitchell: Lady Sasquatch*, 9 Sept.–8 Oct. 2005, Paul Petro Contemporary Art, Toronto. http://www.paulpetro. com/arc/mitchell/2005.php

66 Charles Darwent, 'A mass of contradictions: At once masculine and feminine, monumental and delicate, Roni Horn's *Pink Tons* is an essentially transgender work of art', *Art Quarterly*, Summer 2016, pp.80–1.

67 'Artist Talk – Lynette Yiadom-Boakye and Glenn Ligon, Haus der Kunst, 04.02.16.' https://www.youtube.com/ watch?v=uYfGTa4fUrs, from 47 min 38 sec.

68 Call Out Queen [Mark Aguhar], *Blogging For Brown Gurls*, 4 Jan. 2012. http://calloutqueen.tumblr. com/post/15333639382/calling-things-boring-is-the-best-insult-i-love

69 Self-description from the artist's statement, posted on *UIC [University of Illinois at Chicago] MFA [Master of Fine Arts] Portfolio*, 10 Mar. 2011. http://uicartmfa-blog.tumblr.com/post/3768157187

70 Quoted in Karen Peltier and Brandon Soderberg, 'Edie Fake's *Memory Palaces* bring new life to forgotten queer spaces', *Animal*, 4 Apr. 2014. http://animalnewyork. com/2014/edie-fake/

71 'I carefully select all of the elements of a painting based on my private philosophy of beauty … I can say that I draw and paint only to realise beauty, otherwise I cannot draw any attractive works.' Tomoko Kashiki, 'Artist Tomoko Kashiki on how she paints', *Observer*, 20 Sept. 2009. https://www.theguardian.com/ artanddesign/2009/sep/20/guide-to-painting-tomoko-kashiki

72 Storm Janse van Rensburg, 'Interview with Adejoke Tugbiyele', originally published in Dutch in *Metropolis M*, no.3, Jun./Jul. 2014, pp.81–3. English version at http:// stormprojects.wordpress.com/ biography/adejoke-tugbiyele/

73 Ibid.

74 Stefanie Jason, 'Q&A with Adejoke Tugbiyele: Art that tackles homophobia', *Mail & Guardian* 19 Jun. 2015. http://mg.co.za/ article/2015-06-18-qa-with-adejoke-tugbiyele-art-that-tackles-homophobia

Further reading

General art history

Dominique Fernandez, *A Hidden Love: Art and Homosexuality*, trans. David Radzinowicz, Munich, Berlin, London and New York 2002.

Robert Mills, *Seeing Sodomy in the Middle Ages*, Chicago 2015.

R.B. Parkinson, *A Little Gay History: Desire and Diversity Across the World*, London 2013.

Christopher Reed, *Art and Homosexuality: A History of Ideas*, New York 2011.

James Saslow, *Pictures and Passions: A History of Homosexuality in the Visual Arts*, New York 1999.

Claude J. Summers (ed.), *The Queer Encyclopedia of the Visual Arts*, San Francisco 2004.

Modern and contemporary art

Clare Barlow (ed.), *Queer British Art 1861–1967*, exh. cat., Tate Britain, London 2017.

Tessa Boffin and Jean Fraser (eds.), *Stolen Glances: Lesbians Take Photographs*, London 1991.

Pierre Borhan, *Men for Men: Homoeroticism and Male Homosexuality in the History of Photography, 1840–2006*, London 2007.

David J. Getsy (ed.), *Queer*, Whitechapel: Documents of Contemporary Art, Cambridge, MA 2016.

Gay Gotham: Art and Underground Culture in New York, exh. cat., Museum of the City of New York, New York 2016.

Harmony Hammond, *Lesbian Art in America: A Contemporary History*, New York 2000.

Peter Horne and Reina Lewis (eds.), *Outlooks: Lesbian and Gay Sexualities and Visual Cultures*, London 1996.

Amelia Jones and Erin Silver (eds.), *Otherwise: Imagining Queer Feminist Art Histories*, Manchester 2016.

Catherine Lord and Richard Meyer, *Art and Queer Culture*, London 2013.

Richard Meyer, *Outlaw Representation: Censorship and Homosexuality in Twentieth-Century American Art*, New York 2002.

Derek Conrad Murray, *Queering Post-Black Art: Artists Transforming African-American Identity after Civil Rights*, London and New York 2016.

Michael Petry, *Hidden Histories: 20th Century Male Same Sex Lovers in the Visual Arts*, London 2004.

Cherry Smyth, *Damn Fine Art by New Lesbian Artists*, London and New York 1996.

Acknowledgements

Compiling a book about art you hold dear is a truly delightful occupation, but an author's enthusiasm may not always travel afield. I am profoundly grateful to all the artists and rights holders who generously gave permission for works of art to be reproduced here.

From Tate Publishing, I must thank Jacky Klein for trusting a first-time author and Emma Poulter for coping with the consequences. Emma O'Neill's skilled picture research fulfilled every wish on an optimistic list. Glenn Howard (of Untitled) was responsible for making the end result look this good and Jonas Vanbuel for steering it into the world.

I have lost count of the many kindnesses I have received from colleagues at Tate, but must at least thank Carol Anderson, Jane Bramwell, Holly Callaghan, Jane Carr, Allison Foster, Andrew Gent, Mina Gibaud, Anna Golodnitsky, Maxine Miller and Sophie Risner. Within Tate Digital, Sébastien François and Ros Lawler let me abscond for a whole summer.

For putting me up to this, I owe a particular debt to Clare Barlow. (Are we quits?) Kirstie Beaven, Fionnuala Cavanagh, Camille Gajewski, Chris Griffin, Tony Guillan, Nazmia Jamal and Kee Somasiri have all been exceptionally generous with their time, expertise and comments. Heartfelt thanks are due to Dawn Hoskin, Nadya Kassam, Rebecca Mays, Katy Silverton, and the many friends, colleagues and family members who buoyed my spirits and urged me onwards.

Credits

Page

2 Photo: Morten Pors Fotografi

6 Vingarne © 1916 AB Svensk Filmindustri and Carl Milles © DACS 2017 (sculpture). Photo: Svenska Filminstitutet Biblioteket

10 Harvard Art Museums/Fogg Museum, Gifts for Special Uses Fund, 1955.75 © Photo: Imaging Department © President and Fellows of Harvard College

16–17 © Henrik Olesen. Photo: Courtesy Galerie Buchholz, Berlin/Cologne/New York

18 © Estate of Grace Crowley. Photo: National Gallery of Australia, Canberra / Gift of the Artist / Bridgeman Images

20 © Keltie Ferris; Courtesy of the artist and Mitchell-Innes & Nash, NY

22 © Tejal Shah and Varsha Nair. Photo by Amit Kumar Jain. Courtesy the artist and Barbara Gross Galerie, Munich

24, back cover & 27 akg-images

28–9 Duncan Grant © Tate 2017. Photo: © Tate Photography 2017/Mark Heathcote and Abbie Soanes

31 Robert Montenegro © DACS 2017. Photo: © Victoria and Albert Museum, London

32 Florence Wyle © NGC. Photo: © NGC

35 © Collection: Kent Belenius, Stockholm

36 Marie Laurencin © ADAGP, Paris and DACS, London 2017. Photo: © Tate Photography 2017

38–9 Dame Ethel Walker © Tate. Photo: © Tate Photography 2017

40 Photo: Morten Pors Fotografi

43 Carl Milles © DACS 2017. Photo: © Tate Photography 2017

44–5 © Tate Photography 2017

47 Romaine Brooks © 2016. Smithsonian American Art Museum. Photo: Smithsonian American Art Museum/Art Resource/Scala, Florence

48 Claude Cahun © The estate of the artist. Photo: Courtesy of the Jersey Heritage Collections

51 Edward Burra © Estate of the Artist, c/o Lefevre Fine Art Ltd, London. Photo: © Tate Photography 2017/David Lambert

52 Hannah Höch © DACS 2017. Photo: © 2016 Kunsthaus Zürich

55 Toyen © ADAGP, Paris and DACS, London 2017. Photo: © Moravian Gallery, Brno 55

56 © Tate Photography 2017/Jo Fernandes

58 Amrita Sher-Gil © Estate of the artist. Photo: Courtesy of Vivan and Navina Sundaram. Collection of Vivan and Navina Sundaram, New Delhi

61 Frida Kahlo © Banco de México Diego Rivera Frida Kahlo Museums Trust, Mexico, D.F. / DACS 2017. Private collection. Photo: © Christie's Images / Bridgeman Images

62 James Richmond Barthé © The Estate of the artist. Photo: © The Amistad Center for Art and Culture

65 © Estate of John Craxton. All Rights Reserved, DACS 2017. Photo: © Tate Photography 2017/Mark Heathcote and Abbie Soanes

66 Marlow Moss © reserved. Photo: © Tate Photography 2017

69 Reproduced with the permission of the Ruth Bernhard Archive. Photo: © Trustees of Princeton University

71 © 2017 The Andy Warhol Foundation for the Visual Arts, Inc./ Artists Rights Society (ARS), New York and DACS, London. Photo: Collection of The Andy Warhol Museum, Pittsburgh

72 © Eikoh Hosoe. Photo: YOD Gallery

74 Robert Indiana © 2016 Morgan Art Foundation/Artists Rights. Image courtesy of Simon Salama-Caro Society (ARS), NY / DACS, London

77 © Marisol. DACS, London/VAGA, New York 2017. Digital Image © Whitney Museum, N.Y

78 © David Hockney. Photo: © Tate Photography 2017

80–1 Raúl Martínez © The Estate of the Artist. Colección Museo Nacional de Bellas Artes, Cuba. Cortesía Archivo Raúl Martínez. Fotografía: ©Fernando Fors

82–3 © The Estate of Francis Bacon. All rights reserved. DACS 2017. Photo: © Tate Photography 2017

84 © Zilia Sánchez. Courtesy Galerie Lelong, New York

87 © Barkley L. Hendricks. Courtesy of the artist and Jack Shainman Gallery, New York. Photo: © Tate Photography 2017

88 Carlos Leppe © The artist, Espaivisor Gallery. Photo: Photographic Archives Museo Nacional Centro de Arte Reina Sofía

91 & front cover © The Tee Corinne Papers, Coll. 263, Special Collections and University Archives, University of Oregon Libraries, Eugene, Oregon

92 © Bhupen Khakhar. Photo: © Tate Photography 2017

95 Copyright of Lubaina Himid. Image Courtesy National Museums Liverpool

97 © Joey Terrill. Photo: Joey Terrill

98 © Rotimi Fani-Kayode. Courtesy Autograph ABP. Photo: © Tate Photography 2017/ David Lambert

101 Copyright@2017 Kiss & Tell. Susan Stewart (photographer) in collaboration with Persimmon Blackbridge and Lizard Jones

102 © Nan Goldin. Photo: © Tate Photography 2017/ Joe Humphrys

105 © Glenn Ligon. Image courtesy the artist and Thomas Dane Gallery, London. Collection of the Solomon R. Guggenheim Museum, New York

106 © Ma Liuming. Photo: © Tate Photography 2017/David Lambert

109 © Tracey Moffatt. Courtesy of the artist and Roslyn Oxley9 Gallery, Sydney. Photo: © Tate Photography 2017

111 © Wolfgang Tillmans, courtesy Maureen Paley, London. Photo: © Tate Photography 2017/David Lambert

112 Carmela García © DACS 2017. Photo: Courtesy the artist, Carmela García

115 © Estate of Mrinalini Mukherjee. Photo: © Tate Photography 2017

117 © Zanele Muholi. Courtesy of Stevenson, Cape Town/ Johannesburg and Yancey Richardson, New York. Photo: © Tate Photography 2017

118 © Wangechi Mutu. Courtesy of the artist and Susanne Vielmetter Los Angeles Projects. Photo: Gene Ogam

121 © Henrik Olesen. Photo: © Tate Photography 2017

122 © Karol Radziszewski. Courtesy of the artist and BWA Warszawa

125 © Chi Peng. Courtesy The Artist & M97 Gallery, Shangha

126 © Chitra Ganesh. Image courtesy of the artist 126

129 © AZ / AIF

130 Kiluanji Kia Henda © Courtesy of the artist and Galleria Fonti, Naples

133 © Allyson Mitchell. Photo: Courtesy the artist. Photograph by Cat O'Neill 133

134 © Roni Horn, courtesy the artist and Hauser & Wirth, London. Photo: Genevieve Hanson

137 © Lynette Yiadom-Boakye. Courtesy of the artist, Jack Shainman Gallery, New York, and Covi-Mora, London. Photo: © Tate Photography 2017

138 © Estate of Mark Aguhar. Photo: Courtesy of the Estate of Mark Aguhar

141 © Edie Fake. Photo: Courtesy Edie Fake

142 © Fatima Al Qadiri and Khalid al Gharaballi. Photo: Courtesy the artists

145 Copyright of Tomoko Kashiki. Photo: Courtesy the artist and Ota Fine Arts

146–7 © Adejoke Tugbiyele. Photo: © Courtesy the artist and the October Gallery

149 Athi-Patra Ruga – copyright the Artist, image courtesy of Athi-Patra Ruga and WHATIFTHEWORLD

150 Sadie Benning © Courtesy of the artist, Callicoon Fine Arts, and Susanne Vielmetter Los Angeles Projects. Photography by Chris Austin

Index